Misguided Sensitivity

Philip Nork

Misguided Sensitivity
Copyright © 2012 by Philip Nork

All rights reserved. No part of this book may be reproduced or transmitted in any form or by any means without written permission of the author and publisher.

The views expressed herein are those of the author and do not necessarily reflect those of the publisher.

ISBN: 978-0-9850066-7-9

Library of Congress Control Number: 2012938761

Cover Design by All Things That Matter Press

Published in 2012 by All Things That Matter Press

Previously Published as Sensitivity 101

Foreword

In life each of us is on a journey. It is filled with questions and answers, rights and wrongs; choices and lessons. It often goes by the name "self-discovery." No two lives can ever be totally the same, nor are any two journeys; like fingerprints, yours is totally unique to you. But there is one common bond in all of our paths and that is the presence of other people. How you decide to perceive, interact with, and learn from them greatly shapes the true you that will emerge.

Sometimes how you perceive someone is not exactly what that real person is all about. How they see themselves, in their own mind, can be totally different from how you see them. There are times when you need to look deeper into what is actually happening, since face value does not always equal true meaning. Even when you think you know the truth, a person you meet may change your whole thought process. These people who you meet can change how you think, what you do, and ultimately, who you are.

***

Everything you will read in this book has a basis in truth. However, all names and venues have been changed; and certain events have been either altered or embellished as necessary to honor the participant's wishes for total privacy. But in all instances, the lessons the author learned are valid, and each afforded him the opportunity to change his perspective on how his life has turned out. The author's method of analyzing the effect of other people in his life can serve as a valuable tool to help you interpret how the people you have met influenced who you are today. During this reflection, you will likely envision, as did the author, how you can alter your perception and see yourself in a different light. Perhaps you will even be able to view yourself through the eyes of others and gain an understanding of how they see you. The author's life lessons can also be a great help to you in making peace with some of the choices you have made that perhaps didn't turn out as you would have liked. The best part is, whether or not you participate interactively, in all cases, you will be treated to some very unusual and highly entertaining stories.

Chapter 1 — The Beginning

Every journey has a beginning; this one starts out in a small town southwest of St. Louis, Missouri back in the early 1960's. Times were different back then; it seemed like everything was easier, more enjoyable, and everyone was a lot less competitive. In this town you knew all of your neighbors. As a child you could play outside alone from sunup to sundown. And it was much easier to develop lifelong friendships because there seemed to be a genuine sense of caring amongst everyone. Even though people were more communicative back then, there were still secrets kept which would never come to life. People enjoyed sharing the good times together; for the most part, they kept the bad to themselves.

I was the oldest of three children that my parents brought into this world. As soon as I was born, the people around me knew I was different. I was the center of attention, liked to laugh, enjoyed "moving" to the music, and loved being in the spotlight. I was always told I had a special gift; a natural ability to make others feel good. When my brother was born, three years after me, I had to learn to share the stage. And seven years later, I had to share it even more when my sister was born.

In the 1960's the typical family consisted of a stay-at-home mother, a working father, and some kids. As you grew up you were exposed to an equal amount of boy things and girl things. In my world that never happened. We three kids were raised by a divorced mother and her side of the family. For reasons I did not know, my father deserted the family when I turned eight. He was also on his own journey of self-discovery; it just took him longer than the average man to realize it. He left us kids with a mother who had no skills and no money. Mom could have just given up and slipped into a world of denial. Instead, she decided to learn a trade, get a job, and she tried to give the three of us a decent childhood. In my eight-year-old eyes, she was a hero. Especially between the ages of eight and fifteen my mom was my voice of reason. I idolized her, I respected her, and I hoped to one day marry someone just like her. Between her and her side of the family we were taken care of, loved, and given the nurturing we needed to hopefully become normal, productive adults.

And yet my life took a bad turn after my dad left us. The effects of the separation and eventual divorce felt like it cut deep wounds into my insides. I can remember nights that the four of us would huddle on the couch and cry our eyes out because of what we were feeling. Being the oldest, I naturally took it the hardest. I wanted to help and support both my mom and my brother and sister. Here I was only eight and I was told I was the man of the house now. I always thought I was to blame for my parents' divorce. Because of this, my personality changed drastically. I went from being the center of attention to being extremely introverted, spending hours upon hours alone, in my room listening to music, reading books, and just thinking. The music I liked was not normal for a boy my age. I got absorbed into old country music with its songs about loneliness and hard times. Johnny Cash and Loretta Lynn were my favorites. Even at my young age, I already felt attached to those feelings.

My grandmother was of Bohemian descent and family was very important to her. Although we never heard the words, "I love you" flow from the lips of any family member, we knew that we all cared for each other by the loving symbols that we saw. Her house was full of them, mostly evidenced by the presence of flowers, roses in particular. There were always fresh red roses which meant love and beauty; pink ones for appreciation, yellow ones meaning "I care" and friendship, and most importantly white roses which symbolized remembrance and respect.

But she also warned us all roses have thorns and you need to be careful when handling them or else someone may get hurt. And that people are a lot like roses.

My grandmother also made sure religion and faith had an important role in our life. Because of this, wine—both red and white—also played a big part in our upbringing. She truly believed, "Drinking wine brings you closer to God." And that sign hanging on her dining room wall that read, "God Works in Miraculous Ways," had to be true.

Every Sunday my mom would wake us up early, help us get dressed, and off we'd go to church. We were Catholic, so each week we'd listen to a sermon about what God wanted us to do, how He wanted us to behave, and what was right or wrong. These messages came from a priest who I felt never really understood the meanings. He was an older man, who according to Catholic law, could never marry, never have sex, never have kids, and should never do anything wrong. How could he deliver messages about things he never lived? I sensed this man was not the real deal. I never understood how adults could put so much belief into one religion or one person. Later on, this same priest who taught us about right and wrong was removed from the church for stealing money, drinking, and molesting young altar boys. This was the second man who I felt had failed me in my young life. I always believed there was a higher power, but I had more faith that *what* you did was much more important than the type of building you did it in. I treated people the way I wanted to be treated; I tried to be nice, while also being sensitive to everyone.

After church we'd go back to my grandmother's house for a big dinner with even more extended family. One person I really connected with was my great-grandmother; I called her Nana. The two of us could sit and talk about anything for hours. She'd tell me stories about when she was growing up. At first I didn't believe her when she told me, "We had no television, no electricity, and no indoor plumbing. Living on a farm, there weren't that many other kids around either. I spent most of my time reading and doing chores. My favorite pastime was making noodles with my mom."

There was a feeling I got around Nana I felt nowhere else in my life. It was calming and relaxing. Part of that came from her distinctive smell. It was a woodsy aroma, not really feminine but not overly masculine either. It reminded me of the faint, almost sweet odor of fertilizer. Nana said, "What your nose detects is years of working on a farm and then spending all summer working my gardens to make them beautiful to look at." Whatever it was, it worked on me.

I got along so well with her my mom would let me spend all of my summers with her and my great-grandfather up at the cottage they owned in rural Wisconsin. The smells there were special, too. The air was always filled with fresh cut green grass, the charcoal scents of a hamburger cooked on an open campfire, and the brackish seaweed that lay on the beaches in the early morning. It was a great place for me to be alone with my thoughts. I'd spend most of the morning fishing on the small lake with him, the afternoons lying on the grassy hillside next to the cottage looking aimlessly into the sky, and then the night talking to Nana as we sat in two rocking chairs on the screened-in porch that overlooked the lake. We would share the night by sharing life.

While we sat together, drinking homemade lemonade and eating special sweets that she'd made during the day, Nana became my first exposure to the occult, ESP, UFO's, and the afterlife. Anything others thought of as abnormal was normal to her.

Her lemonade was really the part I enjoyed the most. She always floated a sprig of mint on top. I hated the taste of mint, but loved the smell, so I'd take the sprig out of my glass and put it in my pocket so I could enjoy it later.

On the subject of religion, she reinforced my conviction that it doesn't matter how or where you worship God, as long as you believed. She said, "Treating people with the respect they deserve is the best way to get into heaven."

We also had another ritual which I still do to this day. Whenever the smell of rain came to the air—you know the smell—we would wait excitedly for the storm to hit. As soon as it did, there were the two of us out dancing in the downpour. Nana told me, "Rain is the cleansing agent God sends to wipe away your sins."

She also taught me the first lesson of my journey: You are going to meet many people throughout your life and if you want them to remember you, you must always be a little different, you must be sincere, and you must make them feel special, *especially the girls.*

She died when I was ten and I was devastated. I thought God was punishing me. First He took my father away from me and now He took the only person who truly understood me. I couldn't understand why God would do this. I didn't want to believe in a God who punished people so much. He was supposed to be a good and fair God. Although I desperately wanted to believe in something greater than us, I became confused. This just led me deeper into a life of withdrawal.

While I was going through all this, my mom kept on moving forward. She wouldn't allow anyone to talk bad about my father in the presence of us kids. However, there was one place where she let it all out.

My mom had several friends in our neighborhood. There was the other divorced lady from down the street, the separated lady who lived across the street with her three daughters, some ladies from her chapter of Parents Without Partners, and the lady next door who was widowed. When these ladies all got together to drink and discuss men, after they thought we kids were all asleep, I would listen very intently. They talked about how most men were basically inconsiderate, lazy, and irresponsible. They all had a great distaste for men at this time of their lives and I found I couldn't disagree with them.

I decided right then I never wanted to be a typical man. I was going to do whatever it took to make sure all females liked me, trusted me, and never talked bad about me. I just had no idea how I was going to accomplish that.

But I began to watch the world I was living in more closely. I watched how men and women interacted and realized we were very different. I learned girls like to be in control and plan things out, while guys normally just went with the flow. A man and a woman could hear the same conversation yet never agree on what they had just heard. The women listened to what people said and remembered everything precisely. The men would forget what they heard as soon as they heard it. Men and women would see the same thing happen but perceive it in totally different ways. The women always wanted to help, while a man often chose to ignore. A woman seemed more at ease and asked questions, while a man tried to act like he had all the answers. A woman could talk for hours, while a man would get bored and walk away.

The men I encountered always seemed to be the aggressors. They were loud, short in temper, and fast to place blame. The women seemed more in control of themselves, much more responsible for their actions, and had more trust between each other. Women saw the little things people did and seemed to share more with each other.

After taking all of this in, I needed to know what females wanted from men and how to give it to them. I started to challenge myself to understand things the way a women would. I tried to understand why certain things were so important to them. As I did this, I found myself trusting the females I met more than the males. I knew they had the answers I needed to help me become a better person, or at least one people could trust. I started learning lessons from the females I met and then started piecing together how this boy I wanted to be would look, act, and think.

I remembered how open and carefree I used to be. And I knew the lessons females had to teach me would be my ticket back.

The way people come into your life at precisely the time they do, can make one wonder if our lives are planned out in advance. People seem to arrive just when you need them, or when they need you. And the beauty of it is, sometimes even a small gesture can have a profound effect on you.

Chapter 2 — Jenna

The time between when I was born and when I started fourth grade was pretty normal for me. I was intelligent, funny, and the spotlight was shining directly on me. I was always very short for my age, had a buzz cut, and was the only one in my class who wore glasses. And even though I was smartest boy in class, I was always anxious about how the other kids saw me. I read many books given to me by Nana and liked to share what I read with the other kids and teachers. The guys didn't seem interested, while the girls came to me for answers to all their questions. Even back then the girls knew I would help them with *whatever* they asked me for.

My teachers always treated me the best. They said I was sweet, cute, and very easy to teach. I wasn't like the other boys in class who were into fighting, getting dirty and making fun of people. I just wanted to make friends and be accepted by everyone, especially the girls.

All through first grade I was in the same class as Jenna. She was a short, roundish shaped girl who had a beautiful personality. She was the most popular girl in our class and the prettiest. She had long blonde hair her mom put up in pigtails, and always tied with green ribbons. Jenna had freckles on her nose and under her eyes and always seemed to have a radiating glow around her.

Being we were both smart, Jenna and I were always in the same groups. I often made her laugh with the silly things I did. I had a crush on her but didn't know what to do about it. I remembered the talk Nana and I had about being different, sincere, and making people feel special.

One spring morning, my mom had the radio on during breakfast and the song *Up, Up and Away* came on. It was a catchy tune, even to a six year old, so I found myself humming it on the way to school. When I reached the schoolyard, all of my classmates were waiting outside for the bell to go in. This was my opportunity to make Jenna feel special and to let her know how I felt about her.

Now I wasn't a great singer or even a good one, but I put a lot of feeling into everything I did. I started to sing, "Up, up and away with my beautiful, my beautiful Jenna" to the melody in my head. The other kids looked at me like I was crazy, but Jenna had a cute smile on her face.

I sang this little song every day before school and Jenna would always give me her special smile. It made me feel good inside to be accepted by her. One day during lunch she came up to me, gave me a small hug, and said, "I really like bein' friends."

I learned my great-grandmother was right. If I made someone feel special, was sincere, and was a little different in going about it, people would like me and approve of what I did.

Later in the school year, Jenna had an outdoor birthday party and invited me to come. When I arrived, I couldn't believe my eyes. Her backyard was completely decorated in her favorite color, which was green. There was green crepe paper, green paper hats, and green helium-filled balloons everywhere. Her birthday cake was decorated with green trim and had green icing.

It was a great party and toward the end we gave her presents. Thanks to my grandmother's influence, mine had a yellow silk rose taped to the box. After we had cake and ice cream, her mom wanted to do something special, so she waved all of us kids close to her and explained her plan.

"Everyone get a balloon," she said. "Once everyone has one, we will let them fly into the air and I want you to make a wish." Her intent was to teach us a lesson, and she added, "In life there will be times when you need a friend. Find a friend here today and tie your balloons together, they will fly higher and the chances of your wishes coming true will be better."

Jenna and I immediately decided to tie our balloons together. As they slowly ascended skyward, Jenna smiled at me and said, "I wanna be friends forever." The balloons disappeared from sight and I sang my little song to her while we held hands and agreed to always be friends.

Jenna and I went through the rest of that school year and the next and almost every morning I would sing my little song to her and she would either smile back at me or give me a little hug that said thanks.

Jenna and her family moved away the summer between second and third grade. At the start of third grade, when Jenna didn't show up for class, I was devastated. I didn't know where she moved to or how to get in touch with her. I started to retreat from the other kids. I didn't want to get hurt by getting close to someone else only to have them leave, too.

We changed schools after the sixth grade. By then I was feeling the effects of my parent's divorce and had retreated further into my own little world. Starting school fresh at a junior high was not going to be fun for me, and I was very anxious. There was only one junior high in our town, so all the grade schools combined into this one for the two years before high school started. This is where I ran into Jenna again.

She was standing amidst a group of girls before the first day of school started, talking, and I was very ecstatic to see her again. She still had her freckles and wore her hair in those pigtails with green ribbons, but she had grown. She was taller and skinnier and seemed to be very popular among her new friends. I wanted to say hi to her, but felt very small in the presence of her girlfriends. Not in stature, even though I was still short for my age. I just didn't feel comfortable around crowds of people, especially ones I didn't know. I wanted to make an impression, but not make an idiot out of myself. I thought back to the first lesson Nana had taught me about being different but sincere.

I walked up behind Jenna and said, "Up, up and away, babe."

When she heard those words, she spun around and gave me an incredible hug along with that smile of hers. It hadn't changed throughout the years. It was big, full, and made my heart warm.

One of her friends shot me a strange look and asked, "Jenna, who's the weirdo?"

I was ready to walk away embarrassed. I thought I'd made a mistake approaching Jenna in front of her friends.

To my surprise, Jenna replied very gently, "Leave him alone, he isn't weird. He's a friend."

I smiled, thanked her, and left. Throughout the next two years every time I saw Jenna I repeated my phrase to her. She always gave me her biggest smile in return.

High school came and once again Jenna and I attended the same school. But again we went our separate ways. She had new friends, different interests, and we never hung out in the same groups. Jenna continued to be very popular and, to say the least, I wasn't, nor was I accepted by her new friends. Even though we had drifted apart, every time I would see her, I would say, "up, up and away, babe" and she always smiled back.

Graduation day finally arrived and even though I graduated early, I came back to march with my class. Our class that year was one of the school's largest, around 300 students. Instead of holding the ceremony in the gym, it was held on the football field. They had decorated the field in our school colors, green and white. There were green and white crepe paper streamers everywhere, and on the back of every chair were green and white helium-filled balloons.

We sat through all the ceremonies and finally, after the last diploma was handed out, it was time to celebrate. Normally, that meant the graduates would take off their caps and toss them into the air. This year they were afraid someone would get hurt, so the principal announced he wanted us to celebrate by letting the balloons fly into the air and make a wish that our dreams would come true.

As soon as he finished saying this, I felt a tap on my shoulder. I turned around and there stood Jenna. She asked me, "Do you remember my first grade party when we tied our balloons together and said we'd be friends forever? You were my first friend, and still my best friend."

I've always been a very emotional person, and it became apparent as tears welled up in my eyes.

Jenna asked, "Can we tie our balloons together again like we did back then?"

I nodded and we grabbed two balloons, tied them together and as they flew higher and higher, I began to sing "up, up and away" to her. She smiled her smile I had gotten to depend on so much and kissed me on the cheek.

Jenna looked at me now with tears in her own eyes, and said, "I'll never forget how sweet you've been. It's meant a lot to me. Thanks for being you."

We watched the balloons disappear and realized they were both green in color, just like they were so many years ago at her party.

I had no idea such a small gesture made so long ago could make such a long-lasting impact on someone. Nana was right when she told me to be sincere and to treat the girls special. And by being different, I had cemented a small place in Jenna's life. For a short amount of time, we had become one. We touched each other in ways no one else could relate to. We shared a connection that was as pure as a friendship can be.

I haven't seen Jenna since that day, so I don't know if she still remembers me or not. But every time I see a balloon ascending into the sky, I feel the magic of her smile.

I learned two lessons from this experience:

1) **Be different, sincere, and make females feel special.**
2) **Girls remember and cherish the small things that they experience.**

Chapter 3 — Nancie

Nancie was my second grade teacher's daughter. Her mom brought her into our classroom one day when her kindergarten class had a day off. Nancie was wearing a pink top with pink shorts and pink sandals. Her mom told us she was two years younger than us, but somehow forgot to mention her name.

We quickly learned she was a little shy. Her mom had her call roll so she could get to know each of our names. She slowly got through with this task without looking up and then sat cross-legged on her mom's big chair the rest of the morning. When she crossed her legs the first time, one of her pink sandals fell off and made a distracting noise. This made her sink deeper into the chair and blush a dark shade of red. While she sat there alone, I watched her all morning. She began coloring on a tablet she was holding and didn't look up the whole time.

At lunch, Nancie came out with us, but sat by herself under a tree on the edge of the playground. I decided to go over and talk to her.

"Hi," I said. "I like your pink outfit. You wanna sit and talk?"

She looked me over and finally nodded yes. I could tell she had forgotten my name, so I said, "I'm Phil, and I hope you never forget my name."

She opened up a bit when she replied, "I'll try to remember if you try to remember mine. I'm Nancie, Nancie with an IE."

Nancie and I talked about the morning. When I asked her how she felt about being in our class, she frowned, "I don't like bein' up front. I feel like everyone's starin' at me."

I told her, "I think I know how I can help."

When lunch ended we returned to the classroom. I asked the teacher if Nancie could sit next to me since there was an empty desk, which would make it easier for her to do her coloring on. She asked Nancie what she wanted to do. Nancie gladly came and sat next to me for the rest of the day. She smiled and even got involved with some of the discussions the class had. At the end of the day, she said good-bye to me and thanked me for being so nice.

I didn't give much thought to Nancie after that day.

Fast forward to my junior year of high school. I became a teacher's aide in a freshman English class. Two of my responsibilities had me sitting up front at the teacher's desk grading papers, and taking roll every morning. It was the first day of a new semester and a whole new class of freshmen sat in front of me. I always felt uncomfortable meeting new people and this was no different. I felt like they were all staring at me.

When it came time to call roll, there were some names I couldn't pronounce properly, which made me more nervous than normal. I got through most of the names and then called out "Nancy Ann." From the back of the room a confident voice answered: "Hi, Phil. My name is Nancie, Nancie with an IE."

I looked up and felt immediately at ease. It was Nancie from second grade.

She smiled and said, "You told me not to forget your name and I didn't. After you finish roll why don't you come back here and sit next to me in this empty desk?"

After roll call I made my way to the back row.

Nancie shook my hand and said, "You looked uncomfortable up there. Remember how nice you were to me that day in grade school?"

"Thanks for returning the favor," I replied.

Our situations had been reversed, but the underlying message of this experience remained with me. As a result of my making the effort to reach out, even though it was a small gesture, when years later it was I who needed the help, miraculously it was there.

This was lesson number three, which I added to my list.

1) Be different, sincere, and make females feel special.
2) Girls remember and cherish the small things that they experience.
3) **Girls remember the good things you do for them and want to reciprocate.**

Chapter 4 — Julie D.

Fourth grade started out exactly like every other year. Many of my classmates from third grade and even the teacher remained the same. That meant we knew what the others liked, how smart we were, how each of us would dress every day and what each other would have for lunch. We accepted all of this as normal and it made us feel very comfortable, but that all changed one Monday morning.

When class got settled, our teacher introduced us to a new student, Julie D. She slowly walked into the classroom looking down at the floor and made an immediate impact on the class; unfortunately for her, it was a negative one. She was wearing a white cowgirl outfit and brown cowboy boots, which was anything but normal for our part of Missouri. Julie told us in a very small, quiet voice with a slight Western accent, "I just moved here from Wyoming and I hope we can be friends." I watched her sit down as she picked a seat in the last row. From my perspective, she didn't look at all happy about being here.

For about a week no one in the class made an effort to talk to her. She was always alone and, if possible, became even quieter. She would eat lunch by herself, then go and read books under the same tree where Nancie sat two years earlier. After school she walked home alone, even though there were others, including myself, who walked her way. I surmised she didn't feel at ease here in her new home.

I couldn't understand why no one would talk to her, yet here I was also part of that group. I knew if I were in her shoes I would want someone, anyone to be my friend. I asked my mom why she thought we were all so uncomfortable with talking to Julie.

"The rest of your class has been together so long that you are familiar with each other. Julie's new and a little different—which probably scares some of you," Mom explained. "Not only does she have to make new friends, she's trying to learn new ways of doing things. You should go over and talk to her about something she likes. Watch what she does when she's alone and try to be her friend that way."

The next day after lunch, as I walked over to the big evergreen tree she was sitting under, I noticed Julie was reading an unusual book.

I put on my biggest smile and said, "Hey there, I see you're reading a book about auras. I read about 'em once. My great-grandmother gave it to me. Where'd you get yours?"

Julie looked at me with surprise in her eyes. "My mom gave it to me when we moved here," she quietly replied. "It's to help me figure out who my friends are. If the energy force around you is red or yellow in color, then you'd be a good friend."

Misguided Sensitivity

"So," I ventured, "am I?"

Julie slowly looked me up and down, as if searching for a clue. Then a small smile appeared on her face. "Looks like it," she happily said.

Julie and I started to hang out at lunch, and after school we would walk home together. That's where we talked about auras, UFO's, and far away Wyoming. Through it all, I got the feeling she missed her home and her old friends.

Even though we developed a good friendship, the other kids were still not as nice. One day, while walking home, Julie said dejectedly, "I don't get why the others don't like me. I try to be friendly, but they only ignore me. I just wanna be friends."

"Don't let 'em ruin your life," I replied. "They don't know what they're missing by not gettin' to know you. I'll be your friend for as long as you want me to."

A few months later, a very excited Julie came to school and told the class her family was moving back to Wyoming. As the two of us discussed this on our way home, Julie said to me, "We're all so lonely. Thanks for being my friend. You made my time here a little better."

When we reached her house, she handed me her book about auras, and then a second one and said, "I want you to have my book. It helped me find you and I hope it will bring you new friends. This other book is about trusting your feelings. My mom told me that someday we all may have to make big decisions and that your feelings will never lie to you. She said to trust what they tell you. Anyway, thanks again for being my friend."

When we got to her doorstep, I hugged Julie, watched her open the door, wave good-bye and disappear inside. I never saw or heard from Julie again.

Julie taught me just because someone is different than you are doesn't mean they don't expect the same things in life as you do. A person may look different, you may not have their same beliefs, and sometimes they may even act a little strange, but we all want the same things; to be happy and accepted for who we are.

This lesson was added as number four unto my list.

1) Be different, sincere, and make females feel special.
2) Girls remember and cherish the small things that they experience.
3) Girls remember the good things you do for them and want to reciprocate.
4) **See the difference in everyone and celebrate it.**

Chapter 5 — Lisa & Sally

The years between ages five and eight for me were normal ... well, as normal as could be when you only saw your father on weekends. My parents were separated and definitely had different priorities. My mother's were making a living, keeping a roof over all of our heads, and having food on the table; while my father was just interested in enjoying his life. Apparently, his main idea of that was bowling. He started my brother and me in a youth bowling league when we were very young. At first I wasn't all that interested, but as I grew more introverted, bowling actually was a savior for me. Since it was primarily an individual sport, I could practice alone for hours while getting lost in my thoughts, and still have other people around me.

The Strike It Rich Bowling Alley, in the town next to us, was where I met Lisa and Sally for the first time. It was my first venture outside the comfort zone of school. We were put on the same team that first year. Here I was, smaller than the average first grader, sporting a crew cut style haircut, and wearing dark brown-rimmed glasses.

Lisa didn't look any better. She was a somewhat chunky girl who was a little taller than I was, with long, stringy black hair which was always disheveled. She did have a cute smile, although it revealed a broken left front tooth.

Sally was the biggest of us all. She was clearly overweight, with short blonde hair, and a very distinctive loud laugh. The three of us sure didn't resemble any team I'd ever seen before.

Our team bowled every Saturday morning for twelve years. As our friendship grew we shared many things with each other. But one thing we didn't share was the fact my parents were separated. My dad would pick my brother and me up each Saturday and then spend the morning watching the two of us bowl. Little did Lisa or Sally know that after my brother and I left each Saturday afternoon with him, we wouldn't see our father until the next weekend.

These girls became my first real friends. Through the years others had moved on or moved away, but these two stayed in my life for a long time. As we grew older, we obviously changed both physically and emotionally. We developed our own very distinct opinions, yet we still managed to like and respect each other. The three of us remained together because we had accepted each other a long time earlier for what each of us brought to the table. We stayed friends through good times and bad and were always there every Saturday morning to encourage each other. I learned from Lisa and Sally that friendship is the most important thing you can have in your life. Both of them would play bigger roles in my life later on, but for now we were all plain ol' friends.

This lesson was added as number five to my list.

1) Be different, sincere, and make females feel special.
2) Girls remember and cherish the small things that they experience
3) Girls remember the good things you do for them and want to reciprocate.
4) See the difference in everyone and celebrate it
5) **Friendship is the most important thing, it leads to other opportunities.**

Meanwhile ...

The summer between fourth and fifth grade was, so far, the most difficult time for me. This was when my parents actually got divorced. Lisa and Sally still knew nothing of this. They helped me get through some bad moods, but had no idea what brought them on and never pressed me for details. Our friendships continued to flourish and even though I desperately wanted to let these girls know what had happened, I couldn't bring myself to discuss it. During these times I felt lost and alone, and I didn't want to let anyone too close for the fear something bad would happen to them, which would surely devastate me.

Even though a whirlwind of emotion was raging inside of me, I could only let it out in certain private ways. I spent many nights in my bedroom alone thinking, crying, and losing myself in music. I was really into a musician named Jim Croce, whose music was better to listen to than the old Country and Western songs I used to like. He was much more mainstream and known by other kids my age. I strongly related to a song he sang called *Time in a Bottle*. When Jim sang about "saving each day until eternity" just to spend it with someone, I always thought back to my father before he divorced Mom, and of course Nana. How I wished I could have actually saved those times in a bottle.

A few months after I really started to understand his music, I heard on the radio Jim Croce died. Once again I felt like a man had failed me. But knowing it wasn't really his fault, I took it to mean God was punishing me again. He had taken my father away from us, He then took Nana when she passed away, and now He let Jim die, too. I became even more afraid of getting too close to anyone else.

Chapter 6 — Chuck & Janet

With sixth grade starting my mom tried very hard to help me feel normal. She wanted me to be able to enjoy my childhood and have many friends. Even though I didn't want to, she signed me up for anything that had the involvement of other kids in it. I was already in bowling, so she had me join Little League, the school student council, and finally Boy Scouts. Who would have thought by joining Boy Scouts I would meet a *girl* who could teach me another meaningful lesson? Contrary to the television show, I began to think that *mothers* really know best.

The annual Boy Scout Halloween Party was being held in the gymnasium of our school. We decked out the gym with Halloween decorations and invited all of our families to be part of this celebration. As had become the norm since my parent's divorce, I attended by myself. My mom was too busy with my younger brother and sister to come, and my dad was long gone by this time. But I was getting accustomed to being alone, so this didn't faze me all that much. I figured I would just hang around the other scouts and their families.

One of these scouts was Chuck. He was the #1 jock at our school. He was much taller than the other boys and was by far the best athlete. Chuck was great at basketball, baseball, and especially football. Because of his talents, he also had a pretty girlfriend named Janet. She was a skinny, clean cut girl who had blonde hair and big green eyes. When she looked at you with them it seemed like she could read your mind. The smile she possessed put everyone, including me, at ease even in the most stressful situations. Janet tried to be friends with everyone she met, but Chuck never agreed with this philosophy. He was already under the misconception there had to be cliques in school: geeks and nerds versus jocks and the popular kids. For sure, Chuck didn't want Janet talking to anyone who didn't fit into the latter category.

I was anything but popular or a jock. I was still very small for my age, wore those big, brown-rimmed glasses and was still sporting that crew cut hairstyle. I attempted to play contact sports at school, but I wasn't very good at any of them. I was more interested in how things worked, what people thought about, and how we would all fit into this world together being so different. I guess I didn't need to belong to any clique; I was the really weird guy all by myself.

On the stage that night was a set-up to bob for apples: a gigantic silver bucket filled with icy, cold water and big red apples. As usual, Janet and Chuck were the first ones in line. "I want ya ta get me an apple," Janet challenged him.

Chuck was full of himself and proclaimed loudly, "No problem."

Misguided Sensitivity

I followed right behind him so I could watch this big man on campus get his girl an apple. As Chuck repeatedly tried to stab an apple in his mouth, I started laughing. He continued to miss and everyone could see the frustration set in as his face became red with anger and the sting of the freezing water. Finally Chuck just up and quit. "This is impossible," he bellowed, at no one in particular. "If I can't get one of these apples, nobody else can either."

I was still chuckling to myself when I heard Janet say to me, "Phil, do ya think *you* can get me an apple? Whaddaya say—can you show up ol' Chucky-boy?"

Believing I could, I came up with a smart aleck response. "Yes pretty lady, I can help you."

But I became a little scared after saying that, especially when Chuck glared at me and said, "What makes ya think you can do it, wimp. I'll bet ya can't get any of those stupid apples outta the bucket either."

While I wanted to be the center of attention and prove myself to everyone, I was a little unsure—that is until I looked toward Janet. She flashed me her winning smile, which gave me the confidence to attempt it. I said to Chuck and anyone else who might be listening, "Just watch me."

With the dare being accepted, the other Scouts gathered 'round to see what I could do. I had watched how Chuck tried to do it and I knew I needed to try something totally different. He had attempted to sink his teeth into the apple itself and only succeeded in getting his face wet. I decided to bite at the stems of the apples. Within minutes, I had every apple out of the water and my face was completely dry.

While everyone else clapped and congratulated me, Chuck's temper was boiling over. "How dare ya show me up like that," he barked. "I oughta kick your butt right here and now."

I let out a nervous laugh as I handed Janet the biggest apple and said, "Sometimes being smart beats being strong."

Janet gave me a friendly hug and said, "I knew you could do it. My mom always says not to judge people by their looks, but by what they do. Thanks for the apple ... mind if I call you Stems from now on?"

I gladly accepted her nickname just as Chuck would treasure a first place trophy. As for him, he just shot me a dirty look and stormed out of the gym.

The lesson I learned from Janet made number six on my list.

1) Be different, sincere, and make females feel special.
2) Girls remember and cherish the small things that they experience.
3) Girls remember the good things you do for them and want to reciprocate.

4) See the difference in everyone and celebrate it.
5) Friendship is the most important thing, it leads to other opportunities.
6) **Pay attention to what a person has going on inside, not just their outer appearance or status.**

The Story Continues ...

All through junior high and high school, Janet and Chuck stayed together. Chuck continued to get bigger and stronger and both of them became even more popular. I, on the other hand, continued to sink into my own secret world and, to the kids at school, became weirder and weirder. Every time I would walk past Janet, though, she would shoot me her winning smile and say, "Hi Stems. How's life treatin' ya?"

But before I could answer, Chuck would either storm over, or stare daggers at me from afar. So I would just wink at Janet, then walk away. In my own little way I knew that no matter how many trophies Chuck would win in his life, he would never completely get over that day when I bested him.

Fast Forward ...

About six years after the three of us graduated from high school, a girl I was dating and I were invited to a wedding. The participants were a high school football star from my class and one of the pretty cheerleaders. My date was the bride's hairdresser, which is how we got invited to this social event of the year. When we attended the ceremony I saw all these people who in high school I was afraid of—not to mention didn't have anything in common with, which made me nervous. My date calmed me down, though, and I made it through the wedding.

At the reception, there was a receiving line where you had to congratulate the bride and the groom. Again, I became very nervous. But when I got to the bride, she actually acknowledged me, "Hi, Phil. I bet ya never thought you'd be at my wedding."

I was very surprised she remembered who I was, then quickly realized she knew my date and they'd probably talked about me at some point.

I answered her politely, saying, "No, it wasn't on my list of things to do. I do hope that you're happy and everything works out well for ya, though."

She smiled graciously, said thanks, and then turned to her new husband and asked if he remembered me from school. Of course, he had no idea who I was.

Misguided Sensitivity

My date and I proceeded to look for our dinner table, and as luck would have it, there were Chuck and Janet sitting at the very same one. It was quite understandable they didn't recognize me when we sat down. I had done some growing up since high school. I was now just less than six feet tall, had short brown hair with blond highlights, and wore silver wire-rimmed glasses with black-tinted glass. I also had grown a full beard and mustache.

After we ordered a drink, I asked Chuck, "Whaddaya do for a living?"

He just looked right through me and mumbled, "Uhm ... I'm in construction ... Before I got hurt ... I was very good ..." He continued to talk about his high school football glory days.

As he rambled on, I glanced over at Janet. To me it looked as though she had heard this speech a thousand times before, and the blank stare on her face just confirmed that tonight was one thousand and one. I also noticed the winning smile she once possessed so readily was gone, in place of it was a forced smile which said, "I'm so bored." When Chuck noticed I wasn't listening anymore, he got up and left. This didn't seem to faze Janet at all.

At the end of our meal we were served dessert—a baked cinnamon apple. It sure didn't look at all appealing and it surprised me something like that would be served at such an event as a wedding. The thought of it made me smirk. Janet caught my wry expression and abruptly asked, "What's the look for?"

I turned to her with all the humility I could muster and replied, "I mean no disrespect, I just find it ironic that the first time I met you an apple was involved and you were so alive. Now I see you again, years later, and just like this apple dessert, you're just sittin' there lookin' totally uninterested in life. Excuse me for askin', but what the hell happened?"

Janet began sizing me up. I could see she was studying my features for a clue. Slowly, a smile, her old winning smile, came to her face. "Stems ..." she jumped up, gave me a gigantic hug, "is it really you?"

In an instant we were back in grade school on that big stage during the Halloween party. Her whole demeanor changed and I saw the Janet I remembered resurface.

When I asked what she had been up to, she solemnly replied, "Chuck and I got married right after high school. He was extremely depressed about getting hurt playing football and I thought I could help him reach his other dream. He's a pretty good chef, but won't follow through with it. He'd rather live in the past, rememberin' his good old days, and not focus on what the rest of his life could bring us."

I nodded I understood. "I'm sorry your life didn't turn out the way you thought it should. Would it help if I talked to Chuck? I know a restaurant owner who's lookin' for another chef. I may be able to help ya guys get back on course."

"Why would you want to help us?" Janet looked at me quizzically. "Chuck was never very friendly to you."

"That was a long time ago," I reminded her. "Ya know even though he wasn't that nice to me, you were. You always smiled at me all through school and made me feel appreciated. I'd be doin' this for you more than for him."

Tears appeared in her eyes as she replied, "I see you haven't changed. You always tried to look out for others."

Janet accepted my offer to talk to Chuck and when the two of us stood up to exchange a friendly hug, he picked that exact time to return to the table. His expression made it clear he was mad she was giving rapt attention to someone else and he wanted an explanation.

Janet intervened. "Do you remember a guy from school named 'Stems'?"

"Of course I remember that weirdo," he growled. "Why?"

Janet put a hand on his shoulder to calm him down. "Chuck," she then gestured at me, "this is Stems. I hope you can try to be nice to him because he knows someone that may need a chef, and said he'd be happy to refer you, so *please* be nice."

Chuck was taken aback. He looked me up and down, and then said, "Man, have you grown. Why would you wanna help me, anyway?"

After I told Chuck what Janet and I had been discussing while he was gone, he immediately became interested. I now felt he wasn't as angry or anywhere near as tough as I remembered him to be.

When my date and I were ready to leave, I got their phone number, said I would be in touch, and gave Janet a small kiss on the cheek. When I extended my hand to Chuck, a surprising thing happened. He heartily shook it and said, "I guess you aren't all that weird after all."

Back to Sixth Grade …

The rest of sixth grade was uneventful, by that I mean it didn't happen for me at all. Shortly after Christmas, I developed some mysterious disease. It started with daily headaches in which I would black out and awake in a cold sweat. Constant visits to the doctor provided me no answers. Dr. Marcus felt it was stress related—most likely due to all the things I had been through with my parents' divorce. She wanted me to see a psychologist so I could talk out what was hidden deep inside of me. I'd never felt comfortable talking to anyone I didn't know, so my mom agreed not to make me go.

Misguided Sensitivity

I tried to withstand the headaches for as long as I could and eventually they subsided. But they were immediately replaced by flu-like symptoms and I developed a sharp pain in my lower back. Once again, Dr. Marcus said it was stress related and that she couldn't help me. She gave my mom the telephone number of a specialist, Dr. Paul, and we went to see him.

The first thing Dr. Paul did was give me a total body X-ray. I was put into a coffin-like machine and instructed not to move. The machine transported me through it like a car going through a car wash. Dr. Paul also wanted me to see a psychologist, likewise to release my "inner demons." After a few more tests I found out I had a viral infection which had attacked my kidneys. This is what led to my backaches and the flu symptoms. But he could never find a cause for my headaches.

This was when I started having visions of my beloved Nana, who had been dead now for almost two years. At first, she didn't talk, just walked toward me. But over time, she started leaving me messages.

The one I remember the most vividly was when she walked toward me holding a bouquet of roses, both red and white. "These are for you, my sweet child," Nana smiled. "The white ones will help you remember to be pure of heart and to always have an open mind, while the red ones are to let you know that you are truly loved by God. I know you're having a difficult time right now, but someday it will all come together for you. Though you may not always find the words to express yourself, you can also communicate with symbols to help people understand what words cannot say."

Nana also told me as I continued in this life phase that signs from above would be placed along the way to help me. She wanted me to remember what I saw and put them all together, like pieces of a puzzle. She assured me they would help me find my place in the world.

I wasn't sure if these were dreams or hallucinations brought on my by disease; all I knew was I liked seeing Nana again.

Because of the unknown nature of my disease, I was ordered to stay out of school until the infection disappeared. I spent the rest of the year at home alone, but luckily, I had my homework brought home weekly and was smart enough to keep ahead of the rest of the class, so I graduated with them anyway.

Since I couldn't have any interaction with anyone else, this isolation led me to retreat even more from the other kids. At first I was disappointed I was going to be isolated from the rest of the world, but soon, I began reading more and more. I was interested in just about any subject I could find: medicine, history, psychology, biographies of famous people, Shakespeare—I even found time to read the whole set of the Encyclopedia Britannica. This was where I learned more about roses and their true meanings—like the traditional one for a white rose. It's a symbol of girlhood and innocence, meaning "one who is too young for real love." It also is a sign of secrecy.

In between reading and listening to music, I found some time to think about what type of person I wanted to become. Although I desperately wanted to change my personality, I knew I couldn't. So the next best thing to do was to reinvent my wardrobe, in hopes it would help me regain some of the lost confidence I once possessed. In grade school all the kids dressed basically the same, thanks to our mothers. They picked out our clothes and made sure things matched. I remember thinking out loud, "Women sure have a way with clothes."

You can imagine how all us guys in grade school looked by closing your eyes and picturing Bobby Brady. My clothes were typical of the early 1970's; striped pants in many colors held up by wide belts and paired with big collared, multicolored shirts. My clothes were never the latest styles because my mom couldn't afford brand new things. Most of what I wore were hand-me-downs from neighbor kids or from my uncle on my dad's side. He was just a year older than I was, and was also small for his age, so many of his things fit me. Since most of us kids had been in school together for so long, no one really looked at what you wore anyway.

With the start of seventh grade approaching, I was getting a little anxious. I would be going to a new school, meeting different kids, and would be living out new experiences. I never was very good at meeting new people, although I did warm up after I felt more comfortable around them. So while I was sick and stuck at home, I concocted a fantastic plan on how I would make my mark. I wanted to stand out from the crowd and get the others to approach me. I decided I'd put to use the advice I got from Nana about being different. The more I thought about my plan, the better I felt. It all seemed to work out great in my head, now I just needed to put it into action.

My mom, knowing how important a new start would be for my confidence, saved some money to buy me new clothes. Surprisingly, she decided I should shop for these clothes myself, so the *real me* could come blazing through. But I was lost, I had no idea what went with what, or what I looked good in. That was when I turned to my bowling friend, Lisa.

I called her and explained my situation: "I start seventh grade next week and I wanna be different this year. I need new clothes—will ya help me?"

Lisa loved I had asked her to help, and as we began to discuss my new look, she said, "I like bell-bottoms. Let's find some in different colors. Most of the guys will be wearin' regular 'ol blue jeans so you'll stand out. I know a store that sells black, purple, and gold ones. They also have shiny-material shirts with snap buttons. If you wear bright colored button down shirts instead of t-shirts like the other guys, you'll be even more unique. What colors do you like?"

"Black and silver," I shyly replied. "I know I said I wanted to be different, but I don't want to be that far out."

Lisa agreed with black and silver for school, but made me promise to buy one colorful shirt for bowling.

We went shopping together the next Sunday. My mom dropped us off at the local mall so Lisa and I could begin our mission to turn me into a different person.

We found the pants and the shirts with no problem. After I tried them on, Lisa said, "I really like this. You look older and better put together than any of the other boys I know. Now, you need shoes."

While we walked through the mall to the shoe store we discussed what kind I should get. Lisa suggested, "You're shorter than most of the other kids in school so you need ones that will make ya taller."

I told her I was game.

We found a pair of brown leather ankle-high mini-boots. They weren't exactly boots, but they weren't really shoes either. No matter, they were stylishly different and the soles were three inches thick which added the height I desired.

After exchanging the pants we just bought for ones that fit my new "growth spurt," I once again tried everything on. After I looked in the mirror and then toward Lisa, I knew I had found my new style and that without her help I could never have put this together. I guess girls really do know more about clothes than boys do.

We were leaving the mall when I spotted a florist. The first thing that came to mind were my dreams of Nana and her saying, "Let symbols speak for you when you can't." So I bought Lisa a single pink rose.

When I quietly said, "This is to thank you," I realized it was the first real flower I ever gave to a girl.

***

I was now ready to go and meet my new schoolmates. Monday morning I got all decked out in my new clothes and was feeling somewhat good about myself. Since this was the first time I had ever been in my new school, I got lost and walked in late to class. As I looked around at a sea of new faces, I lost my confidence and became extremely nervous. I could feel the sweat start to run down my face as reality hit me: I knew no one in this class. Not one of my prior friends, or even enemies, were here. As I scanned the room for a place to sit, I tripped over my new bell-bottoms and fell right into one of the girls sitting in the front row. While I tried to regain my composure I heard someone call out, "Look at the weirdo. The guy doesn't know how to walk *or* how to dress."

The laughter and cat-calls lingered in my ears as my face turned a bright shade of red. I apologized profusely to the girl I practically landed on, then found my way to a desk in the back of the room. I slumped into the chair trying to make myself as small as I could. In a totally different way than I expected, I had followed through on my plan to be different and get noticed. I thought I would never live down my "grand entrance."

Later in the day, I did run into one of my previous classmates, but she didn't recognize me. Having missed most of sixth grade, I had changed drastically. I now was a little over five feet tall, still small compared to the other guys, but getting closer. Gone was my crew cut, replaced by shoulder length brown hair that I parted down the middle. Gone also were my old glasses replaced by silver wire-rims. But these changes only affected my outside appearance. I remained the same quiet, insecure guy I had been since my parents' divorce. I still had a very difficult time talking to others until I knew them and unfortunately, I never seemed to get to know anyone.

I had the hardest time talking to girls. I would stammer and start to sweat when one of them would say anything to me. But I did know how to listen.

I was putting my books away in my hall locker at the end of the first day when I overheard a conversation between two girls who were standing at their lockers across and down the hall a short way, and apparently thought they were out of earshot.

"There's that guy that fell on me in class today," the tall, blonde in a cheerleader outfit said. "He seems like a strange one."

"No kidding." The short red-headed beauty chuckled; then she became serious. "Outside, before school, I called him a weirdo … but then Jenna said they were friends."

"Jenna likes him?" the blonde reconsidered. "Wow, ya know, as he was apologizin' to me I sensed somethin' about him … I can't quite put my finger on it. Here's this clumsy, oddly dressed kid, practically layin' in my lap and I wasn't offended I really didn't mind."

The redhead shrugged. "I don't care about any of that stuff. All I know is that he's really cute."

Chapter 7 — Barbara & Claire

I needed to do something quickly about the fact I couldn't feel comfortable talking to others, so I decided to switch one of my classes for a drama class. I liked the idea of acting because it allowed me the luxury of pretending to be someone else. I was always good at that — I just wasn't good at being me yet.

The first person I met was Barbara, actually, she was my teacher. Right from the start, she sensed I was different. In class I was always very quiet until I was told to portray someone else. As soon as I became that character, my personality changed drastically. I was much more comfortable and suddenly I was the center of attention, just like before the divorce.

Barbara saw how I came to life when in character and said, "Phil, you have a talent that you need to experiment with. You're a good actor. You should be in the school play."

"No, I can't." I blushed. "I'm way too scared to get in front of all those people."

Barbara kept egging me on until one day when she decided to show me something. She introduced me to a girl named Claire. Like me, Claire also was very introverted, had small anxiety attacks when she met new people, and preferred keeping to herself. She was a big girl with short, red hair; many freckles peppered her face. When I first met her, I noticed she had the most beautiful green eyes, which were always darting around as though she were trying to take everything in and didn't want to miss anything. I felt instantly relaxed when I looked into them.

Claire was very good at pretending to be someone else. One day Barbara asked her to get up in front of the class and do a monologue she'd been rehearsing. Claire exuded a captivating presence from within when she started reciting her lines. She was in complete control of the room and at ease with herself. She was finally someone she could believe in.

Barbara and I were standing at the back of the classroom. While Claire performed, Barbara asked me, "How do you like Claire's technique?"

"She has a way about her. She's very comfortable with being a different person and it shows," I replied. "She looks in total control, and everyone seems to like her more."

"Phil," Barbara whispered to me, "you're twice as good as she is when you are in character. Both of you are introverted, not only in how you react to others right now, but how you process information. You both keep important things inside instead of letting them out, and this will hurt you in the long run. You must begin to let your emotions out, whether that means you write a short poem, shoot a beautiful picture with your camera, or possibly even act in a play." Barbara winked as she said that. "Learn to let go more and really express your feelings. People will look at you differently when you do." Then she got to the point, "I'd like you both to be in the school play."

Claire finished to rousing applause, then joined Barbara and me.

I looked into Claire's green eyes and said, "I'll do the play if you will."

She grinned and agreed.

Thanks to Barbara, both Claire and I were big hits in the play that year. I was concerned at first because my big scene had me crying, and I didn't know if I could do it on cue. Much to my surprise, when the time came for me to cry, I thought about how my dad made me feel when he left us, and the tears came flowing down.

Barbara was right, after the play some of the kids did start treating Claire and me differently. Neither one of us was ever totally accepted, but I knew I felt better about myself than I had in a long time. I thanked Barbara and Claire by giving them both a pink rose. They told me it was a sweet gesture and Barbara even told me she fully understood the underlying hidden symbol behind it. It looked like I was breaking through.

The biggest change, however, was that some of the girls who had seen the play started to approach me. With them broaching the conversation, it became easier for me to interact with them. All of them mentioned the fact I wasn't afraid to cry made them feel more comfortable with me somehow.

Thanks to Barbara and Claire lesson number seven became:

1) Be different, sincere, and make females feel special.
2) Girls remember and cherish the small things that they experience.
3) Girls remember the good things you do for them and want to reciprocate.
4) See the difference in everyone and celebrate it
5) Friendship is the most important thing, it leads to other opportunities.
6) Pay attention to what a person has going on inside, not just their outer appearance or status.
7) **Allow your emotions to show others you are open and caring.**

On with the Story…

I began feeling a little more comfortable at school since I finally had

Misguided Sensitivity

some girls talking to me, and many more who had at least heard of me. I figured this was a good time to take advantage of my new found confidence, so I decided to try out for the boy's basketball team. This would be the first team sport I tried to play since little league baseball, not including bowling. This was different since it was all boys I didn't know.

Well, all the momentum and confidence I gained from being in the play disappeared the first day of try-outs. I was very nervous standing on the gym floor in my raggedy white shorts and gray t-shirt with a few holes in it. I had old sneakers on that had seen better days, while all the other boys wore orange shorts and black shirts, as our school mascot was a tiger; and they all had expensive looking new basketball shoes.

The coach, a big loud-mouthed former semi-pro athlete, called us to the free throw line by blowing on the whistle which hardly ever left his mouth. As we lined up, I got lost between the rest of the guys. I was a little over five feet tall while most of the others were well past that. I managed to squeeze to the front of the line where the basketballs were laying in a semi-circle on the floor. I bent over to pick one up and, just my luck, the one I reached for was coming apart at the seams. The old leather had been ripped and was just barely hanging together. Instead of grasping the whole ball with both hands, I held the ball with one hand by the loose piece of leather. When the coach saw this, he stormed over to me, spat the whistle from his mouth and started yelling in my face. He was so close I felt his spit hit me on the nose.

He started with, "What are ya doing holdin' the ball that way? Do ya think we're made of money and can afford all new ones? Who taught you how to hold a basketball, anyway?"

When I tried to answer him, he just yelled louder. He looked me up and down and continued his tirade. "Just why are you here? This isn't the try-outs for cheer-leading ya know, this is for boys' basketball. You aren't man enough to be on my team."

The other guys started laughing. I was so ashamed I started to cry and I quickly ran down to the locker room. Once again a man had failed to understand or try to help me.

I changed clothes and got out of that awful place, heading back upstairs to my locker to get my homework. After I reached the hallway, I realized the doorway was closed. I had no idea they locked the hallways after school. I panicked and began crying once more. I wanted to go ask the coach how to get through, but with the state I was in and the bad impression I had made, I decided not to. I sat down and waited in front of the locked fencing until I saw another teacher pass by. Luckily it was Barbara. She wanted to know what happened and as I explained, she found the janitor who opened the door for me.

I decided that was the end of my basketball career, and I tried to forget about the whole thing; but the guys who were on the team weren't about to let me. They would point at me and laugh whenever and wherever they had a chance. I found out the hard way, guys weren't as impressed with the ability to cry as girls were.

This especially didn't help me to change my introverted ways, and I retreated to the individual activities I felt comfortable with; like listening to music and taking pictures.

It took the entire year for me to live down the basketball debacle. In eighth grade I decided to try out for soccer, obviously I was much too small for football. It was an intramural team so everyone who tried out made it. I wasn't extremely fast and I definitely wasn't big, so the coach made me the goalie. It turned out I was actually quite good, despite my size. The team played every day after school and even started to get a small following. The girls who didn't like football began watching us. Many of these girls knew me from the play. They started to talk to me in the halls with more regularity and I was beginning to get a small "fan club" which made me feel very good. And when the school year ended, I actually had some good friends, both boys and girls who truly understood me. They thought I was a good actor and—who would have guessed—an even better soccer player. I had a ray of hope high school might not be another torture for me.

Chapter 8 — Faith

Freshman year started and once again I was feeling my insecurities flaring up. I had to start all over with a new school, meeting different kids, encountering new teachers and their classes. It seemed like every time I started to feel comfortable in my life and come out a little, something else would come up and drive me back into my shell.

Due to my experience in junior high, one of the new classes I was put in was an advanced drama class ... only this one was for seniors. Talk about being miscast. Here I was an insecure freshman, basically a child, put into a room full of near-adults ready to graduate.

The teacher, Mr. Jackson, after saying we should call him Joe, asked us each to stand up and introduce ourselves. The others all stood up brimming with confidence and talked proudly about who they were and why there were in this particular class. When I stood up and nothing came out of my mouth; these older adults just stared.

Eventually Joe asked, "Are you sure you're in the right class? This is drama, which means you have to talk — get your feelings out."

I had to do something or, once again, I would start out with a bad reputation. I just had no idea what it was.

That's how I met Faith. She was sitting right behind me and whispered, "Do your monologue from the play you were in ... in junior high."

I glanced at her, at first confused, but quickly composed myself and launched into my character. As soon as I made the change, all the confidence I needed came through. I did my entire monologue and ended it the way I did in the play, by crying real tears.

After the class stood up and clapped for me, Joe said, "I guess you are in the right class after all. Now, who are you?"

I laughed, but stayed in character, and said, "I'm Phil, a freshman, and somehow I was put into this advanced class by mistake. I'm glad ya think I belong, but I believe I'm in way over my head."

Faith responded, "Phil, you're stayin' right here."

The rest of the class voiced their agreement.

Class started and I still felt out of place. At the first break several of the other students came over and complimented me on my performance. Since I wasn't in character, and was just being me, I felt my responses came across as uncomfortable and clumsy.

Once again, Faith came to my rescue. After class she approached me and asked, "Hey, Phil can we talk for a minute?"

I timidly agreed and we moved to where the kids hung out between classes. I was very nervous, but rather happy other freshmen saw me talking to a senior—a senior girl at that.

"I saw your performance in junior high," she said. "My kid sister was also in that play. You were great, so in control, especially the way you turned on and off your emotions. Why don't you have the same confidence in yourself as you do when you're playing someone else?"

Sheepishly I shrugged my shoulders. "I guess I don't have anythin' to offer to people as Phil. I just don't believe in myself yet."

She looked at me in amazement. "Phil, my sister told me all about you. You have a gift—when you act it makes people feel good. Let me help you to get that same result when you are just you."

Faith and I met daily after school to work on building the confidence I lacked as "me." We role-played different scenarios; she put me on the spot and pushed me to my limits. When I proceeded to get more comfortable with her, she brought in some of her friends to help. The more we did this, the more relaxed I felt being me. I didn't change drastically, but did feel myself changing inside; maybe the belief I did have something to offer was beginning to shine through.

I couldn't believe Faith, a senior, would help me, a younger guy, find myself. Whenever I asked her about our age difference, she would say, "Age doesn't mean a thing except passage of time. When you're lucky enough to find someone you connect with, someone who needs your help, regardless of how old they are, you should explore it. You never know what you may learn yourself in the process."

After this important lesson I gave Faith two roses, a yellow one and a red one. The yellow was for friendship and the red was because I thought I was in love with her. I was in seventh heaven, an older girl liked me. This was my first realization there was someone or something watching over us who sent help when we needed it. I remembered the sign hanging in my grandmother's dining room which read, "God Works in Miraculous Ways."

Two weeks after letting her into my heart, Faith was killed in a car accident. I couldn't help but believe I was to blame as some of the other people I had let close to me, my dad and Nana just to name two, also ended up being taken away from me in some way or another.

At her wake, as I cried out loud without embarrassment, I gently laid a dozen roses next to her, eleven pink; in appreciation of her help, and one dark lavender, the closest I could find to black, as a fond farewell to what we had shared together.

In memory of Faith, I added number eight to my list:

1) Be different, sincere, and make females feel special.
2) Girls remember and cherish the small things that they experience

3) Girls remember the good things you do for them and want to reciprocate.
4) See the difference in everyone and celebrate it
5) Friendship is the most important thing, it leads to other opportunities.
6) Pay attention to what a person has going on inside, not just their outer appearance or status.
7) Allow your emotions to show others you are open and caring.
8) **When you truly connect with someone, age does not matter.**

Getting back on track …

The rest of my freshmen year continued and I began to slowly open up, but still had my silent moments. Inside I felt like no one knew who I was. Soccer helped me get noticed, and when I became the starting goalie, this helped boost my confidence. And an incident which happened at one of those games helped move that to an even higher level.

Many people didn't even know we had a soccer team. We practiced and played at a local school called The Third Street Elementary School rather than on the big football field at our high school. One day my mom came to watch me play and was one of only ten people in the stands. Among them were five girls who sat together. She overheard them trying to recognize the players, but being freshmen and not knowing who was who, they didn't know many of us by name.

Once I stopped a shot, one of the girls got all excited and said to her friends, "I know him, that's Phil. We went to grade school and junior high together. He's a little shy, but check him out, isn't he cute?"

The other girls looked my way and agreed with her. When I passed by them after the game, my mom heard one of them chirp, "He really is kinda cute. Let's come to all the games and watch him play."

This comment made my mom smile and helped her feel a littler better about me. She only knew the person she saw at home, the one who was all about staying in my room alone, listening to music, and not talking to anyone. After she retold this story to me, I asked, "Who were those girls, what did they look like, and which one liked me the best?"

Unfortunately for me she had no definitive answers.

Chapter 9 — Terri

I decided to spend the summer between freshman and sophomore years with my great-grandfather, who I called Gramps, at his cottage by the lake. The whole place made me feel good to be me again. I really reacted to the cottage, the smells of the lake, and the memories of Nana. I was able to relive some of the special moments Nana and I shared, like running around in the rain and drinking ice cold lemonade. Although I never added mint to mine, there was plenty of the leafy substance in the kitchen, as Gramps thoroughly enjoyed floating a sprig on top of his lemonade, just like Nana always did. The smell of it made me realize just how comforting it was to me. I swear, at night I could almost feel Nana next to me as I sat in one of the rocking chairs overlooking the dark lake. I began to look forward to the nights because they let me remember one of the few people I really felt understood me. I truly missed Nana, but could sense her spirit near.

I used most of my free time learning how to take better black and white photographs. I concentrated on using my emotions, and those of my retired senior citizen subjects, to tell a story. The more I practiced, the better I became. I found out even pictures of flowers or the sky had a story to tell and that I had a real knack for making them all come to life. This came in handy as I was made the number one photographer for the school newspaper, *The Weekly Beat*, when I returned for sophomore year.

I showed the editor some of my pictures from over the summer and she immediately assigned me the job of taking pictures of the cheerleading squad. I was extremely nervous about this assignment since the cheerleaders were two things which made me antsy; they were popular girls and very pretty. These weren't senior citizens sitting on their porches the editor wanted me to take pictures of.

She told me to go and meet with the head cheerleader to get started. When I initially approached Terri, who was almost six feet tall, I could almost read her mind as she looked down at me. I imagined she was saying to herself, *Why'd they send this squirt to do a man's job?*

In addition to her height, Terri had long brunette hair while her eyes were big and brown. When I first looked into them I felt like she was staring right through me. I felt the sweat begin to bead up on my forehead. Terri also had curves exactly where a girl should have curves. This made me blush as I felt my eyes start moving down toward her chest, unable to stay focused on her eyes.

Terri took the lead right from the start and I could tell she liked to be in control. She gave me specific directions on how she wanted me to shoot the pictures; all I had to do was listen and follow them. Due to all

Misguided Sensitivity

the distractions, her enormous chest for one, my mind wandered in and out, and her directions didn't set in my mind all that well. When Terri stopped talking, she asked if I was ready. I shrugged my sagging shoulders and shyly nodded yes.

I went on my way to photograph the ten most beautiful girls in the school. When I approached them, I could feel their eyes looking right through me, as if I should know I didn't belong on their turf. Instead of talking to them, I just started snapping pictures. As hard as I tried, I couldn't get the same feelings from them as I did from my senior citizen subjects all summer long. The pictures I took seemed posed and unfeeling. I knew there were no good stories emitting from them like I knew I could get. The only story these pictures told were that the shoot went terrible.

I now had to go back to Terri and explain what happened. She listened to me stammer and watched me sweat for a few minutes before I saw a change in her. She seemed to loosen up as she put her finger up to my mouth as if to silence me. Just like a teacher would, she explained, "Your problem is two-fold. The first thing ya did wrong was that you didn't actually hear me. I know I gave you precise instructions on what to do, and you basically ignored me. I'm going to let ya in on a little secret; a girl really wants a guy to listen to her. She wants you to remember what she said, but more importantly, she truly wants you to understand what she implied. We sometimes talk in code, ya know. Your second problem was that you didn't get the girls to trust you. You need to go slow around girls and watch closely what their eyes say to you. A girl's eyes will begin to sparkle as they begin to trust you. When you see that look, you're in like Flint."

The more she explained, the more I listened. Terri continued to become much nicer as she went on. When she looked into my eyes as she talked, I suddenly felt a connection between us. I saw her big brown eyes begin to invite me in, not look right through me, like the first time I met her. In fact, she gently said, "You have a certain softness in your eyes, one which tells me that you're a nice guy. You should use that to your advantage when you meet a new girl. You have a calming effect about you that I know other girls will surely feel."

While those words came flowing from her mouth, I saw the sparkle she told me about come to life in her very own eyes.

I asked Terri if I could go back and try again. When she agreed I was ready, I went off with a new found confidence. I first approached Bailey, one of the prettiest cheerleaders, and slowly started to talk to her. I didn't feel nervous at all. After I explained the shot I wanted to take of her, I asked her why she liked cheer-leading. Bailey started talking back, so I made it a point to listen intently to what she said. I nodded my head to acknowledge I heard her, repeated some of her answers, and I looked directly into her eyes. The more I responded to Bailey, the more she loosened up. She started talking "to me" instead of "at me." I began to snap pictures of her in action and soon was able to enjoy the sparkle I wanted to see in both the pictures *and* in her eyes. The more she smiled and had fun, the better her pictures became. This led to all the other cheerleaders gathering around me to get their pictures taken, too. After they began to accept me in their sacred world, everything with the second shoot went smoothly.

I was feeling very happy about myself; it was a wonderful surge of warmth, like the feeling you get from doing a good deed, flowing through my heart. I didn't know what it was, but it sure felt great.

Terri and her friends had become my acquaintances, not really my friends, but close enough for me. They all came up to me individually after the shoot and said I was a nice, sincere boy. They said they felt very comfortable around me and because of that, I was able to ignite the sparkle in each of their eyes. When all of them agreed I had made them feel special, Nana came to mind.

I bought a bouquet of beautiful pink roses the next afternoon and gave each cheerleader one as a thank you for helping me break through my shell.

I added numbers nine and ten to my list.

1) Be different, sincere, and make females feel special.
2) Girls remember and cherish the small things that they experience
3) Girls remember the good things you do for them and want to reciprocate.
4) See the difference in everyone and celebrate it
5) Friendship is the most important thing, it leads to other opportunities.
6) Pay attention to what a person has going on inside, not just their outer appearance or status.
7) Allow your emotions to show others you are open and caring.
8) When you truly connect with someone, age does not matter.
9) **Girls want to be heard; guys need to be better listeners.**
10) **Girls show their trust by a sparkle in their eye.**

Intermission

I had set out on a journey back when I was younger to find out how to be a male that females respected. I didn't want to be like the majority of men I encountered or heard about. When I started on my mission, I had no idea how to achieve it, but with help from my Nana, and some of the nicest girls I met along the way, I now had the secret formula. They taught me the ten basic lessons which would help me continue on my way.

I made a promise to myself, *I would use these ten lessons, and any others I would learn, to help myself grow and find myself,* just like Nana said. I would add each piece of the puzzle whenever I could. My ultimate goal was to use what others called my gift, the gift to help others feel good, purposefully.

I would focus on being a male all females I met wanted to keep as a friend, and one who they fully trusted. Hopefully, Nana would continue to be there to help me along the way, although I was sure there would become a time I would have to make my own decisions regarding what was and what wasn't really a lesson at all.

I was still far from being the man I wanted to be, so for the first time in my life, I actually prayed to God I was going about this correctly. But knowing my track record, there were going to be some unexpected twists and turns along the way.

Chapter 10 — Lisa, Redux

There was a feeling of change coming over me, mostly physically. Thanks to the weight training involved in soccer, I added some definition to my previously skinny body frame. My lower body became extremely toned, especially my long legs, and my twenty-nine inch waist. I was now just less than six feet tall and had let my hair grow past shoulder length, which I tied in a ponytail during my soccer games. Hair also started growing in places where it never had before, like under my lip and on my now well-defined chest. All this made me feel much more masculine than I had in the past.

Although all these physical changes were happening to me, mentally I was still an introvert at heart who continued to be shy around the girls at school. There were two significant events in particular that happened within a few months of each other which helped me grow emotionally.

The first one was the success of the soccer team. We had gone undefeated as freshmen and began to have a bigger following. We started sophomore year winning our first seven games and the football team wasn't winning at all, so we started to see more people attend our games.

Our team moved from the small field at the Third Street Elementary School to playing our games on the big football field right on campus. As more people showed up, the more we won. All of us basked in the spotlight we were suddenly in. But being the starting goalie, I got most of the attention. I had girls from all grades coming up to me in the hallways wanting to talk to me. Luckily this made initial meetings much easier for me, since I still couldn't approach a girl on my own. However, this new found attention also made life a little more difficult; I had a hard time remembering them all by name. My natural reaction became smiling and winking back at them. I also heard through the grapevine my name started coming up in the girl's locker room in a way I had never thought about before—sexually. At that time I had no idea what to make of it.

I was slowly regaining the carefree attitude I enjoyed before my parent's divorce, but it was still going to be a long ride before I discovered how to take advantage of it.

The second event which happened involved getting my driver's license. The power and freedom of driving allowed me to feel I was in complete control for the first time in my life. Along with this privilege came my first car. I was able to buy a used 1969 Plymouth Road Runner. It was teal in color, had an adjustable sliding front bench seat, and being made in Detroit, was put together with the strongest US steel available. I bought a mint scented air freshener and proudly hung it from my rearview mirror, as this car of mine, after my room, soon became my second safe haven. I also bought a brand new cassette player and had it installed so I could listen to my favorite music when I needed to. I was now able to relax and think in both my room *and* my car. Having this vehicle and my license, I became more in demand than ever before. However, being the skeptic I was, it made me wonder whether people liked me for being me or only because I could drive them where they wanted to go.

Getting my license really changed my life for the better when it allowed me the experience of my first date. Yes, here I was, about to be a sophomore in high school and had never been on a date before. Even though I had been told I had this gift to make girls feel good, I really never knew how to use it to my advantage ... that all changed one afternoon after bowling.

Lisa, Sally, and I were talking about nothing in particular that afternoon. Somehow the subject of dating came up and we realized none of us had actually been on one yet. This wasn't all that hard to understand considering who we were.

Even though I had changed physically, I was still emotionally immature.

Lisa had changed the most from the first time I met her. She had grown into a tall, lanky girl. All the baby fat she once carried seemed to have melted away. She learned how to use makeup and knew what the best hairstyle for her was. Her black hair was now long, down to her waist, and she washed it every night. Lisa never went out without looking perfect. The only reminisce of her younger days that didn't change was that broken tooth, revealed whenever she smiled.

Sally, on the other hand, hadn't changed at all. She was still overweight, loud, and continued to have that obnoxious "Woody Woodpecker" laugh. She did have a very pretty face, though, which complimented her other not-so-pretty features.

Through all these physical changes, the three of us were still able to stay friends because, regardless of these changes, we had accepted each other for what we were long ago.

When I asked them what their perfect first date would be like, Sally answered me rather dryly, "I just wanna go a movie or maybe to dinner. I really haven't thought too much about dating. When it happens, it happens."

Lisa, on the other hand, had hers all planned out. "I wanna romantic drive out into the country where the two of us could talk and learn about each other. Followed by a slow, long walk around a lake, and finally end up with a fantastic kiss that I'll never forget."

As she was saying this, I swear I saw her eyes begin to sparkle, just like Terri taught me to look for. I knew what I had to do.

I waited until Sally walked away for a minute and quickly asked,

"Lisa, how about us goin' on a date? We've known each other for nine years now, so it should be rather easy for us. I trust you, you trust me, and I think we should experience this together."

Lisa produced a great big smile. She shook her head yes and said, "I'll have to ask my mom first. I'm sure she'll let me since she knows you. I'll call ya later tonight so we can plan this momentous occasion."

That wasn't as hard as I thought it would be. I asked a friend to share some special time together and she agreed. If only I could talk to other girls the way I could talk to Lisa.

I was a little nervous the rest of the day. I had a habit of imagining the worst and this time was no different. My stomach was tied up in knots up until the phone rang that night. When it finally did, the real nervousness set in. My hands got clammy and my heart started beating through my chest, but somehow I still answered it. I didn't even get the word "hi" out when Lisa excitedly exclaimed, "I can go, but my mom wants us to double date for safety reasons."

I didn't even hear the last part after the words "I can go." This experience just confirmed some of the ten lessons I learned really worked. I was always sincere when dealing with Lisa. I had seen what she had inside, ignoring her appearance at first. I became friends with her; I listened, and finally got to see her eyes sparkle.

"I don't think we should ask Sally to double with us though, it would be too uncomfortable," Lisa said. "How about I ask one of my friends from my school and you ask someone you know from your school?"

"I can ask my friend Billy. You and Sally met him at bowling last season, but he is a year younger than us," I replied. "Do ya think that'll be okay?"

After Lisa agreed, we hung up so I could call Billy and she could call her friend. I told her I'd call her back as soon as I talked to him. I searched my memory and remembered what Lisa said about wanting to go to the country on her first date; but with a double date I wasn't sure how to make it happen. What I did come up with was the next best thing. I outlined the planned date to Billy and after he agreed with it, I called Lisa to let her know about it, too.

"*Leese*," I announced confidently, "we're gonna have a picnic next Saturday after bowling. We'll go to Redwoods, the forest preserve out by my house, have some lunch, and get to experience each other outside the bowling alley. How's that sound?"

She was definitely excited and said she couldn't wait.

The week went by so slowly. I couldn't concentrate in school; all I could think about was my first date. When Saturday finally arrived, I was the most nervous I'd ever been. I wanted to look sharp for Lisa, but didn't know what to wear. When I turned on my newly purchased Air

Misguided Sensitivity

Supply record to help calm me down, I remembered which outfit was her favorite. I put on a pair of newly purchased dark purple bell-bottom jeans and a golden yellow shirt like she had picked out for me. When I went into the bathroom to comb my hair and put it in a ponytail, I looked into the mirror and was very pleased with the guy I saw looking back at me.

After picking up Billy, we started talking about the date the whole way to the bowling alley. Billy was a little nervous because this was his first blind date. When he asked me, "What's this girl look like?" I shrugged my shoulders and replied, "I dunno, I've never met her either. I'm sure if she's a friend of Lisa's, she must be good lookin'. Lisa doesn't hang around ugly people."

Billy laughed and said, "What about Sally?"

I rolled my eyes at him and said, "She's not ugly, she's just big. She has a very pretty face and her heart is in the right place. You can't always judge a book by its cover you know."

***

Bowling was a total disaster for both Lisa and I because we were both so nervous.

Afterward, she called her friend so her mom could drop her off. While Lisa waited at the alleys for her to arrive, Billy and I went to get some food from the local Schnuck's grocery store for the picnic. When we returned, Lisa introduced us both to Mary. She was one of the most beautiful girls either Billy or I had ever seen. She was a short little thing, about five-foot-two, black, shoulder length hair held up by a colorful red scarf, and her teeth were perfectly white. She reminded me of the cheerleaders I photographed at school.

As with any girl I was meeting for first time, I was my typical clumsy, awkward self. I started to sweat and when I tried to talk, my voice just squeaked out a barely audible hello. She smiled at me and said I was cute.

I wasn't sure, but thought maybe she wasn't all that thrilled with Billy—perhaps because he looked so much younger than his age.

After we all got into the car for the ride to the forest preserve, Lisa was surprised by a yellow rose on her side of the seat. I noticed her and Mary look at each other and smile. After the girls and Billy began talking to each other, all I could do was listen. I couldn't have talked anyway as my throat was so dry from my nervousness. When *All Out of Love* came on the radio, I heard Mary say, "I really like Air Supply. You know, they're comin' in concert pretty soon."

As soon as she said that, I immediately calmed down and was able to join in. "You like Air Supply? So do I. I really like their slow ballads with their great lyrics. It's like, I can relate to what they're sayin'. Their songs are all about tryin' to find love, and the feelings you get when you lose it. If you read in between the lines, many of their songs are very dark. This lets their hidden feelings emerge without anyone really knowin' the truth, although they do imply many things that most people don't understand. I wish that I could write a song or somethin' that expresses what I truly feel."

Mary looked at me and said, "You can do anything you put your mind to. Even if no one else feels the same way about it, it'll always mean something to you."

I filed that thought away in the back of my mind. Someday I would write something others could fully relate to.

We finally arrived at Redwoods and located the perfect place for a picnic. We sat high on a big, grassy hill which overlooked the lake below. From up there you could smell the water, hamburgers of other picnickers cooking in the air, and the freshly cut green grass. I immediately felt comfortable, as it reminded me of Gramps's cottage up in Wisconsin. Things were going smoothly and as I glanced at the girls, I saw the same sparkle Terri told me about come to both their eyes. I didn't know if the one coming from Mary's eyes were meant for me or Billy and was too afraid to ask.

After eating, Billy suggested he and Mary go for a walk. Before they took off, Mary turned and winked at us. I think it was directed at Lisa and meant to say everything was fine and good luck. As soon as they disappeared, Lisa and I started talking.

"Well, I hope this fits the criteria of your perfect first date so far," I smiled. "You said ya wanted a drive to the country. Does this count?"

Lisa beamed. "Yes, this does count as the country. I can't believe you remembered that."

"Good," I said, "I learned to be a better listener from a friend of mine at school."

"You're totally different than you are at bowling." Lisa relaxed, sat back and continued, "You always seem detached there, but here you're much more at ease. You seem to care about only me right now. The rose was sweet and I know Mary also thought it was a nice touch."

"My great-grandmother taught me in order to make an impression I had to be a little different." I shrugged. "This place reminds me of a summer cottage she lived at in Wisconsin, so it makes feel very comfortable. And my grandmother used to have roses in her house all the time. She said that a yellow rose means 'a special friendship.' I hope I'm your special friend."

Lisa winked and nodded yes.

"Now, let's get the second part of your perfect date taken care of." I said standing, then holding out my hand to help her up. "How about we take a walk around the lake?"

While we walked, I let Lisa do most of the talking. I just wanted to listen, learn, and remember. "I have four brothers and no sisters," she told me. "I feel so out of place since I have no women in my life, except my mom, to learn from or share things with. Ya know, my parents are having some major problems and I haven't got anyone to talk to about how it makes me feel. I really think they're going to end up in a divorce and I don't know what that'll mean to me."

I felt for Lisa and wanted her to know I cared. "Leese, I'll always be here for ya. You can share anything with me. In fact, I wanna share somethin' with you. This is very hard for me to say, but I know how you feel about your parents' problems. My parents got divorced seven years ago and I know how it has affected me. Let me be there for ya when ya need someone to talk to."

Lisa was stunned. "I had no idea that your parents were divorced. I see them both at bowling, but now that you told me, I realize they're never there at the same time. Why'd you hide this from everyone?"

I blushed, shrugging my shoulders. "I'm not really hiding it; I just don't talk about it. I'm very good at masking many of my true feelings. I don't believe in sharin' personal stuff with strangers."

Lisa and I sat down to continue talking about these "adult" issues. We shared many things that day. We cried, we laughed, and we became closer than ever before. On the way back to our picnic spot on the hill, Lisa and I held hands and smiled a lot. We had made a brand new connection, one which greatly intensified our friendship. It became one where trust and understanding were the foundation.

For the second time I could remember, I felt a small surge of warmth flow through my heart and I couldn't help but wonder if this was God working in a miraculous way.

When we returned to the picnic spot, we saw Mary and Billy also had made a small connection—enough to want to date again on Friday night. Mary said, "I've always wanted to try to roller skate, why don't the four of us go to The Roller Wheel, that rink down by the Mississippi River?" We all eagerly agreed.

When I dropped Mary off at her house, Billy decided to walk her to the front door, which left Lisa and me alone again. Lisa looked at me with a hopeful look radiating from her eyes and said, "Well, two of the three things I wanted on my first date have come true. I've had a great time so far, and I hope that the third piece of my wish happens, too. That would really make me feel good."

My mind raced back to sixth grade and the smart aleck remark I said to Janet at the Halloween party. I changed the meaning a little, as I said,

"Yes, pretty lady, I can help you feel good."

Thanks to my lessons, I now knew that *every* lady was going to be pretty to me in their own special way. Nonetheless, I started to blush and get nervous. Lisa saw the change and thought it was cute.

After Billy returned and I drove him to his house, I started planning in my head what to do when Lisa and I got to her place. We finally arrived and I got out first to open her car door. While we walked together to the front door, I became extremely nervous again. I felt like I always did whenever I met a new girl, all sweaty and stammering. Lisa sensed this, looked me in the eyes and said, "I had a great time and we shared a lot today. I can't wait for Friday night to get here." With that she stepped forward and gave me a big, incredible hug.

I wanted to kiss her so badly and even though she made the first move, I couldn't muster up the confidence I needed. I gave her a weak hug back, told her I'd call her later and then sheepishly walked back to my car.

All the way home I continued to review my first date. I believed, for the most part, it went well. I had another one coming on Friday, but couldn't help but feel bad for not being able to kiss Lisa. I wanted to make her feel good, but just couldn't summon up the confidence to follow through.

I called her later that night and started out by saying, "I'm so sorry I couldn't make your perfect first date come true. I just got stuck. I've never kissed a girl before and I didn't know how to do it the right way. I wanted to so badly, but I just couldn't. I feel so bad for lettin' ya down. Can you ever forgive me?"

I felt Lisa smile through the phone when she replied, "Phil, we're friends and always will be. The date was as perfect as I needed right now. Someday you'll understand that not everything needs to be perfect to be considered good. What we experienced was a good thing and I'm sure God is happy with how you handled it, as I am." She paused a moment then said, "You know, you don't always have to give in to what others want. Start thinkin' about yourself ... and by the way, I cannot wait until Friday night."

I'd taken a big step in my growth. I had used most of the ten lessons I learned to successfully navigate my first date, and set up a second. I was excited and couldn't wait until Friday night either.

***

Friday night finally arrived and I wanted to look my best. I wore gold jeans paired with my black pullover shirt. Once again, I put my hair in a ponytail. When Billy and I picked up the girls, they both looked great.

They had tight blue jeans and concert t-shirts on. Mary was wearing Air Supply, while Lisa had on Aerosmith. I noticed right away Mary had a bigger chest than Lisa, and I was caught looking at her. Luckily, Mary didn't let Lisa know she saw me staring.

As we drove the final mile to the skating rink, we noticed directly to our right was the Mississippi River, which ran parallel with the road. We continued toward The Roller Wheel Rink and we saw many cars parked in a certain area along the bank, with couples inside the cars huddled together, and I asked, "I wonder what happens there?" Mary laughed and said that it looked like a good place to hang out and "do what comes naturally."

Soon a large neon sign began to take shape in the distance. The closer we got to the rink the better we were able to read the sign which lit up the night sky: *At the Roller Wheel spend some quality time together!* Like the kids in the parked cars, we hoped to.

***

We were all excited when we walked into the skating rink. None of us had ever been here before and had no idea what to expect. What we saw was a big concrete floor covered with polyurethane that made it shiny. The surrounding floor had carpet with benches all around facing toward the rink. Lights blinked on and off in perfect rhythm with the dance music, which was blaring in the background. The atmosphere was electric to me and I strangely felt right at home from the start.

The four of us changed into our gray rental skates and as soon as we stood up, we all fell down. Luckily, the floor below us was carpeted to cushion the blow; and since we didn't know anyone else anyway, we all laughed, helped each other up, and proceeded to go onto the big rink.

The place was jammed, which made our first time around the rink even harder. Mary held on to Billy while Lisa clung to me. Slowly we made it around the rink. Eventually we got the hang of it and started enjoying ourselves. The music was good, the company was good, and the night went by too fast.

***

After dropping off Mary, and then Billy, I drove to Lisa's house. This time I knew I'd have enough confidence to give her the kiss she missed out on at the end of our last date. Once again I opened her car door and we walked up to the front door hand in hand. Just as I was about to kiss her, the front porch light flared on. It startled us both. The front door flew open and there stood her mother in a panic. She was crying and told Lisa she needed to talk to her right away. Once again, I didn't get to give Lisa her kiss.

Lisa called me later that night, crying. She apologized for what happened on the doorstep and then said, "Phil, my worst nightmare just happened. My parents *are* getting a divorce. I don't know what to do, can we talk?"

I let Lisa get it all out. I listened and when she cried, I cried with her. We shared another monumental time together. When she was all cried out, Lisa said, "Thanks for bein' there for me from the start. I'm so glad you're my friend. It feels like we can share anything with each other. Thanks for tonight, and for listenin' to me. I owe you one."

After our phone call, I felt that small surge of warmth in my heart again. I liked the feeling and hoped to experience it more often. I took it to mean I had done something good.

***

The next day was Saturday and that meant bowling. Billy decided to come with me so we could discuss the night before. On the way to the alley, we agreed these double dates should become a regular Friday night routine.

Lisa and I greeted each other with a long, slow hug. She again thanked me for last night. After asking about a standing Friday date, she promised she would first call Mary and then me later that night.

But Lisa didn't call that night. It was the following Wednesday before I heard from her. When I asked why, she replied, "Phil, I have something to tell ya ... we can't double anymore with Mary and Billy. Now don't say anything yet, but Mary feels uncomfortable cuz she likes you better than she likes Billy."

I was a little confused and asked, "What's that mean?"

"Well, Mary and I were talkin' at school about you," Lisa said. "She really likes you a lot and since you both have so much in common, I think you should go out on a date with her."

Now even though I had learned some great lessons, I knew I was still extremely naive about things like dating and girls, so for the first time in my life I realized *girls* talk to each other about boys, just like the older women did about men.

"Are you serious?" I shook my head in disbelief. "What about us? I thought we were getting' along just fine."

"We do get along real well," Lisa calmly replied. "I just think we're better off as friends. Mary and you are perfect together in a different way. I told ya before I owed you one; well this is my way of returnin' that favor. We'll always be friends, no matter what happens. Anyway, it's just a date ... it's not like you're gonna fall in love with her and get married or anything."

*****

Up until now I've only shown you *my* side of what's happening. To be fair, I believe the women should have "equal time." So in this, and other italicized passages to follow, you'll get to hear their version of the same stories.

I first met Phil when we were just kids. We were put on the same bowling team and stayed on it for years and years. He was always friendly and had a knack for helping others and making them feel good about themselves. He was quiet when you first met him, but opened up as he got to know you better. He always listened to you and wanted to help out any way he could. Most of the girls at bowling wanted to date him, but he didn't seem interested. When he heard me describe my 'perfect first date' he asked me out. We shared many things on that first date and we connected in a special way.

After the first couple of dates, I realized Phil and I were better off as friends. He was fun, he was nice, and he was sensitive ... everything a girl could want. But with all the changes I had to endure with my parent's divorce, I knew I couldn't spend enough time with him. He deserved much more than I could ever offer. Mary didn't have to say anything—I could tell she was just tolerating Billy so she could be around Phil. So I told her they should go out.

Chapter 11 — Mary (My first real girlfriend)

Once again I was feeling nervous and scared, but knew I must follow through with this opportunity. But before I could talk to Mary, I needed to square things with Billy. As far as he knew, they were an item — but obviously Mary wasn't feeling the same.

"Hey, man," I said when Billy picked up the phone, "I've got a problem and need your help."

"So, what's up?"

"Look we can't double anymore."

"Why?"

"There's a small situation —"

"Yea, what's that, man?"

"Well …" I hesitated, and then let it out, "Lisa says Mary wants to go out with me."

"Lisa said that?"

"Yeah, Lisa's cool with it, but I'm concerned about you. I don't wanna lose our friendship over a girl. So if —"

"Yeah know, that's just fine, I tried to kiss her after the last date, and when she wouldn't let me I could tell she wasn't that into me," he said. "There's many more fish in the ocean for me to troll for. So go ahead and have some fun, we're cool!"

I laughed, thanked him, and hung up. When your friend can make a joke about you stealing his girlfriend, you know he's going to be just fine.

I thought calling Billy would be hard but now I had to muster all my confidence and call Mary. To help me think I put Air Supply on my record player, sat back on my bed, and practiced making the call. I even went as far as to put the phone to my ear while holding down the receiver button. While I listened to *Come What May*, I looked into my mirror and did the impossible, I dialed Mary's number. When it started to ring, I thought I should just hang up and forget all about this. My heart was racing and I was petrified.

The phone rang again and then a third time. I thought I was saved, but lo and behold Mary answered it on the fourth ring. All my practicing went straight out the window when I squeaked out a small hello. I heard a voice on the other end but couldn't make out what she was saying. I had forgotten the record player was on so loud. I quickly got up, turned down the volume, and said hello again, this time in a more controlled voice.

"Is that Air Supply in the background?" Mary sounded a little surprised.

"Yeah, it is," I replied, gaining a little more confidence. "I always listen to 'em when I get nervous. It normally relaxes me, but it's not really workin' this time."

"Why are you so nervous around me?" Mary laughed. "I'm nothin' special. I should be nervous around you, based on what Lisa says."

"I'm sure she exaggerates," I offered.

Mary continued on with all the nice things Lisa said about me and I closed my eyes to listen to her more intently, but started to imagine her in my mind instead and remembered everything about her. I could see her big, brown eyes. Her shoulder length black hair was held up by that colorful red scarf. I was able to picture her beautiful smile. Those big, pearly white teeth, which were all straight and perfect, smiled directly at me. In my mind, she was wearing her tight blue jeans and had on little white sneakers. When I pictured this beauty, I wondered what she saw in me.

We talked for hours, well mostly she talked and I just listened. Mary had a great passion for talking. She just continued on and on like the Energizer Bunny, "I'm the oldest of three kids; I'm a cheerleader at school, well, not a cheerleader, but a pom-pom girl; I really like dancing, movies, and Italian food; I've dated about ten other guys, but never really felt like they liked me for who I was, only for what I was; I saw the way you treated Lisa and liked it. I sense that you're kind and you're the best listener I have ever met."

I had to be, even if I wanted to talk, there was no way I could get a word in edge-wise. When she finally took a breath and there was moment of silence, I made the best of it. I asked Mary out for the following Friday.

She quickly answered back, "I'd love to, *but* you need to meet my parents first. When I'm not on a double-date with a girlfriend they know, they wanna feel the guy out first."

I immediately suggested, "Why don't you set this up for next Wednesday after dinner?"

Mary seemed pleased at my eagerness, but also surprised. "None of the other guys wanted to meet them so quickly."

"I don't especially wanna, either, but I can tell this is important to you."

Mary laughed and said, "I appreciate your honesty, but believe me, they'll love you."

But as I hung up I found myself worrying. Famous last words?

***

The rest of the week went by slowly as all I could do was think about meeting Mary's parents. I tried to picture in my mind how I would act, what I would say, and how I would hopefully impress them. However, I could only think about the worst things that could happen instead, like possibly leaving my fly open, or passing gas inside their house, or God-forbid—they would ask about my parents.

Finally, Wednesday night arrived and I found myself relatively calm. I took a shower, then put on my best clothes. I decided to wear a version of Lisa's favorite outfit of purple jeans and the golden yellow shirt. They worked for her and I was hoping they would work tonight.

Around my neck was a gold tiger pendant I had gotten one Christmas from my dad. It showed up in the mail and since it was the only bond I shared with him, I wore it every day. Because of the pendant and because of the hair on my chest, I chose to leave the top two buttons of my shirt undone. Instead of wearing the shoes Lisa picked out, I put on a pair of black cowboy boots. While I combed my hair, I decided to let it hang down freely—no ponytail. After shaking it dry, I looked into the mirror and hoped I could pass the "parent test."

I got into my car, turned on the radio, and went to meet the parents. The closer I got to Mary's house, the more the anxiety built. I felt my hands become clammy, I got a lump in my throat, and I started sweating. When I pulled into the driveway, the nervousness became dramatically worse. I actually had to sit in the car after I turned off the motor in order to regain my composure. I closed my eyes and tried to picture Mary and her smile. As this remarkable picture of her developed in my mind, I relaxed, took a deep breath, and then approached the front door.

After ringing the bell, I heard her panicky voice in the background saying, "Please don't embarrass me, he's a great guy." With that, the door opened … and there stood her father.

He was a big man. Now, I was just under six feet tall, but I felt like I came up to his waist. His shoulders were twice the size of mine and when he extended his hand for me to shake I was sure mine would get lost inside his. Talk about being intimidated, the sweat started coming down my face again, and my hands got so clammy I didn't want to shake his back. I tried to, but all he got was a limp wet mess. This was not how I had planned it in my mind, so I began to think about what I was going to do after being unceremoniously put out into the night, as I was sure I had blown my chance at dating his precious daughter.

Mary had mysteriously disappeared; leaving me to fend for myself with this goliath. I clumsily followed him into the living room where he told me to sit down on the couch. He seemed so serious and hadn't even cracked a smile yet. He silently continued looking me over like a farmer looks at a cow just before he slaughters it for his dinner.

He said, very monotone, "How'd you meet my daughter?"

"Um … through Lisa at the Strike It Rich Bowling Alleys," I explained very uneasily.

Then he narrowed his gaze, "And what are your intentions?"

Intentions, I had no intentions, in fact I didn't even know what intentions were. I just shrugged.

Finally, he said, "Ya know, I've always wanted my daughter to date a football star. Are you a football star?"

I had a flashback to eighth grade basketball tryouts and how the big, burly coach made me feel. I just sat there as his stare burrowed right through me. I didn't want to answer and I couldn't move.

With that he slowly started to crack a small smile, and then he let out a thunderous laugh. He slapped me on the knee and said, "Relax man, I'm just kiddin' with ya. Mary told me that you'd be extremely nervous, this being your first *real* date and all. I just wanted to make sure ya never forgot it."

The more he eased up, I found myself liking this man more and more. Mary's dad became the first man I actually trusted. I also realized there was scent in the house which was familiar to me: the faint smell of mint. It made me relax even more as I felt Nana was with me the whole way.

We were both laughing when Mary and her mom finally walked into the room. I remembered an old movie where I saw a gentleman stand up when a lady walked into the room, so that's what I did. I marched right up to her mom, held out my hand, which was no longer clammy or wet, and said, "It's a pleasure to meet you, ma'am."

She returned the gesture and looked at Mary, winked and mouthed to her, "Nice start," and "What a dresser."

She sat down next to me and starting asking questions. Normally I was more of a listener, but knew this time I had to become the talker. When she asked me about school and my future, she seemed impressed when I replied, "Right now I'm a straight A student. I'd like to parlay that into either going to Northwestern University to study photo-journalism or get a soccer scholarship to the country's best soccer school, San Diego State University."

The questions continued and I became more comfortable being around this family. Then it happened. Her mom asked me about my parents and what my dad did for a living. I started to panic and got real quiet. I sat there staring into nothingness when her mom smiled gently and said if she was getting too personal, I didn't have to answer.

I shook my head no, took a deep breath, and for the first time to total strangers said, "This is a difficult subject for me cuz my parents are divorced ... have been for a long time. I don't even know my dad that well."

Minute tears welled up in my eyes, so Mary's mom put her arm around my shoulder and tried to comfort me, "That must've been a tough thing to say. I know divorce isn't all that common, but you seem to be very well adjusted and you were brought up well, that's for sure. Your mother must be something special."

I breathed a sigh of relief and the roller coaster of emotions I was on ended. Mary and I would be going out on our date come Friday.

Driving home that night, I had time to think about what happened with Mary's parents, and earlier with Billy, so I added lesson number 11 to my list.

11) Always tell the truth and you won't have to keep track of all the lies you told.

***

Mary and I went to a movie on Friday night. I picked her up, said hello to her parents, and we were off to the local theater to meet some of her school friends. I seemed to be accepted by them; at least they didn't reject me right off the bat. I have no idea what movie we saw as my mind was in outer space the whole time. I was so proud of myself. I had met a beautiful, popular girl who liked me for being me. I was accepted by her family *and* her friends. I couldn't have been happier.

After the movie, I drove Mary back home. I climbed out of the car first, opened her door, and then we held hands as we approached her front porch. She began talking and I began stalling. Mary had been on many dates before and knew exactly what was expected, while I had no idea. The whole time she was talking, I was busy thinking: should I kiss her, how do I go about kissing her, and if I actually do get to kiss her, how will it be? I got myself so worked up Mary sensed something was wrong. She put her hands on each of my shoulders, looked me straight in the eyes, and said, "In order for this relationship to work we need to be honest with each other. I know somethin' is goin' on in that head of yours, so what is it?"

I remembered my recent vow to tell the truth and said, "I'm debatin' on whether or not to give you a goodnight kiss. I don't even know if ya expect one. I need some help here."

With that, Mary grabbed the back of my neck, pulled herself in and kissed me, long and soft. My whole body first went limp, then stiffened in shock as the adrenaline rush flowed through it. I pulled back from Mary, looked into her eyes, and weakly said, "Wow, that was my first kiss ever. It was better than I could ever have imagined. How was it for you?"

"For a first kiss it was acceptable. We'll have plenty of time to work on techniques later." She smiled and added, "You're such a nice guy. You

Misguided Sensitivity

thought about me and my feelings before you acted upon yours. The other boys I dated never did that. They couldn't care less what the girl felt, but not you, you're sensitive and you've made me feel real good tonight. I hope I did the same for you."

I drove home in a daze as I replayed the entire week in my head. I listened to Lisa and dated someone new without losing her as a friend. I'd been accepted by this new girl, her family, and her friends. I also received my first kiss, all by using the lessons I learned. My confidence was at an all time high. For the first time in my life, I actually thought God might be on my side.

When Phil called me I was surprised. He was dating Lisa and I thought they were great together. When I told Lisa about my feelings for him I thought she would be mad, instead, she suggested I go out with him. I thought she was just being nice, but when he called me I learned she was sincere. After talking to him, I was glad he called me. He was so different from the other boys I normally went out with. He was quiet, sensitive, and later, actually liked my parents. I remember the first time they met him. My dad tried to play the big tough guy, which was the furthest thing from his personality. He had Phil sweating for a while, but let him off the hook. My mom liked him right from the start. She liked the way he dressed and his politeness. She especially liked his honesty.

That first date was something. I could tell he was nervous at first but then he settled down. My friends liked him, too. He got nervous again as we sat talking on my front porch after the date. We were there for two hours before I kissed him. I didn't think he was going to kiss me and I wanted one. When we finally did, I knew it was his first without him having to tell me, which he actually did. He was honest and so naive when he asked me to critique his first kiss. And he was so unlike any other boy I've dated, I found myself liking him more.

Being that he was so innocent, and I surely wasn't, I thought about what other new experiences we could share together. I had an idea what they would be, and wasn't too sure how Phil would take to them. But I knew that by the time I was through with him, he'd be a different person.

Over the next two months Mary and I went on the normal type of dates such as roller skating and to the movies. We spent most of our time at a local 24-hour restaurant called Round the Clock, which happened to serve the best lasagna I ever tasted. Since Mary liked Italian food so much, this became our special retreat where Mary and I could sit for hours and talk about anything.

So for a change of pace, I planned a special night for Mary—with some help from a friend of mine, Tim, who worked at the local radio station. When I picked her up I said, "Tonight we're doing somethin' different—I'm in charge. I'm tellin' ya now it'll be a long ride. I don't wanna hear the words 'where are we going?' So just sit back, listen to some music, and enjoy the ride. I'll let ya know when we get there."

Mary did what she was told, but clearly didn't like it. Like most girls, she preferred being in control. When we were a few blocks from the "secret location," I told her to close her eyes and keep them closed, promising her she was in for the night of her life. She did so, albeit reluctantly. I pulled into the parking lot, jumped out of my car, opened her door, grabbed her hand, and she followed my lead into the building. When we were standing in the main room, I said, "Now you can open your eyes. Look around and tell me where we are."

Mary scanned the area, but had no idea.

I gave her a hint, "Look over there, do you see the two guitars on the stage?"

Mary just looked at me, dumbfounded. I escorted her to the front row, lifted the program off her seat, and showed her the note attached to it: "The all new Golf Mill Theater-In-The-Round proudly presents Air Supply in concert, and welcomes Mary and Phil to experience them in the finest seats we have."

Mary almost fainted; she looked at me with tears of joy in her eyes, and exclaimed, "This is the concert I always wanted to see. But I forgot all about it. How'd you remember?"

"I try to never forget anything you've said to me."

When the concert started and the stage began to turn ever so slowly, Mary was in seventh heaven. When Air Supply started to sing *Two Less Lonely People in the World,* which was her favorite song of theirs, she squeezed my arm so tight I almost yelled out.

After the show, Tim arranged for us to get backstage passes; so not only did Mary get to hear her dream band, she got to meet them in person.

Who would have thought just by paying attention to a girl's offhand wish that such a night could happen?

I casually mentioned the first time I met Phil that I wanted to see Air Supply in concert, and then I totally forgot about it. It seemed as though he liked them, too, since he was always listening to their records in his room when we talked on the phone. I never imagined he would remember about the concert. I was very surprised at that, not to mention the way he went about making it so special for me. Being able to meet my favorite band was just unbelievable.

I was feeling a little down before I met Phil and meeting him actually brought to life the lyrics of Two Less Lonely People in the World. Because of Phil, the two of us were no longer lonely. He helped me get over the loneliness I was feeling and made every day seem better. He was still the sweetest and most sensitive guy I ever met, but there was something missing.

Misguided Sensitivity

He was naive about relationships and what should happen. I didn't let it bother me though, I still enjoyed being with him and, especially that night, he made me feel like a queen. Now it's my turn to make him feel like a king.

***

During this time with Mary, I stopped talking to Lisa, not really intentionally, but more due to the fact bowling had ended. One April night Mary and I decided to go to a local carnival. While we were walking hand in hand, smiling and laughing, we ran into Lisa. When my eyes met hers I had no idea how to react. She knew Mary and I were dating and were happy, but this was the first time she had seen us together. Mary and Lisa made some small talk, while I just stood there feeling awkward. Lisa must have sensed this because she came up with a lame excuse about meeting some friends and needing to leave. She then gave me a small hug, and whispered in my ear, "I'm so glad you're happy. I told ya that you guys were made for each other."

As I watched her walk away, in spite of what she said, I thought I had done something wrong. This wasn't supposed to happen; I was the one who was supposed to make the girls feel good, not bad. Mary and I continued on with our night, but I wasn't the same. I started thinking, *I wish I had a sign from above; and I hoped I would be forgiven.*

Just as I was feeling my lowest, when Mary and I walked to the car, there started a gentle rain. I smiled to myself and knew somehow it would all work out.

***

I was beginning to feel a change come over me while I dated Mary. Whenever I was around her, I felt more in control of myself, I walked a little faster, and stood a little taller. I noticed I could talk to other girls without stammering or sweating. Without Mary around, at school, I was back to being the same old guy; extremely quiet, never voicing my opinions, and once again unable to initiate conversations with girls. That's when it hit me, the confidence I gained was directly related to having a girl by my side. When Mary was standing next to me I temporarily lost my own identity, I became "Mary's boyfriend," which was just like acting. Since I was 'someone else' around Mary, I was able to relax more.

I also saw the people around us, especially the girls, acted differently as well. There were many times when Mary and I were together another girl would come directly up to me and start talking. And I knew I could feel the waitresses give me more attention when Mary and I went out to eat, but didn't yet understand why it was that way.

***

While Mary and I were experiencing many new things, the one thing we didn't experience was having sex. But this was *my* idea, not hers. My religious upbringing and the fears the priest had put into my head about good and bad, and heaven and hell, made me want to wait until I got married … if even then. Mary never understood this part of me and thought I was just scared. To be totally honest, that may have been the real reason.

Mary and I hugged, kissed, and even started having heavy petting sessions together. She desperately wanted to expand the physical part of the relationship, while I was happy with just the emotional connection. I often told her, "You put way too much emphasis on the physical. Why can't we just be together?"

I always left these discussions the same way I came into them; wondering why sex was so important to her and it wasn't to me.

I never understood why Phil wouldn't have sex with me. He gave me some lame excuse about wanting to wait until he got married and quoted some religious garbage. I knew he was inexperienced, but wasn't it the girl who wanted to wait, not the guy? I had urges you know. I tried to respect his decision, yet never fully understood it. I did what I had to do to make my urges go away, but he never caught on. I made it my mission to have sex with him; I was going to repay him for the concert night he gave me, but instead of introducing him to Air Supply I was going to introduce him to the promised land.

***

Even though Mary knew I wouldn't give in on this subject, she took it upon herself to help me learn about sex. She started out with the finer points of French kissing. Mary said, "The way you kiss tells a lot about how you feel toward the other person. Let's work on makin' your tongue an instrument of pleasure."

She kissed me softly and said, "Girls like a guy to take their time and we have certain areas you should focus on. Let me show you how to excite these sensitive areas—like the roof of my mouth, the base of my gums, and my lips themselves. Don't ever forget to spend time makin' a girl feel good about who she is."

I kissed her the way she explained and after she sighed, she added, "There are even more sensitive areas around my ears and my neck you need to know about. If you're not gonna have sex with me, *at least* make me feel good with how you kiss me."

I found myself saying, "Yes pretty lady, I can help you feel good."

I continued to learn and Mary would encourage me and let me know when I was improving. One night she remarked, "I can feel your tongue getting stronger and more in control every night. You've passed step one, now onto something new and exciting, for both of us."

Mary proceeded to take off her top and then taught me how to touch her breasts and nipples 'the way a girl likes them to be touched.'

She also shared, "Most guys, when given the chance to touch breasts, are honkers and dialers. They'll attack the breast and start grabbin' at 'em like they were bicycle horns. That doesn't feel good to a girl. Then when they get to touch a nipple, they act like they're tunin' the dial of a radio knob. Again, this doesn't feel good; it takes away all the enjoyment for the girl."

She gently kissed me, and then took control. "This is what I want you to do; slowly cup my breast in your hand and use the art of anticipation to slowly and gently touch me with one finger very lightly. Circle around my nipple with the same finger and as I start to react to your touch, slowly squeeze it between that finger and your thumb until the nipple gets hard. This is what feels good to a girl, not the attack mode most boys use."

After practicing and passing this test as well, Mary then commanded me to put it all together. She then explained to me how to use my tongue on her breasts and nipples. She said, "This is what a girl wants from a guy. You feel good *and* so does she. I have other sensitive areas on my body your tongue will make feel good, too, like the tips of my fingers, the inside of my palms, and around my belly button."

After more practice sessions, Mary finally told me I was now 'her little pleasure maker.' She said, "I have much more to teach you, but you're getting very good at what ya do know."

I loved using what she taught me, but that was as far as I would let myself go with Mary.

***

While I was learning all about Mary's body, she also taught me things about mine. With all this practicing going on, you can imagine what I was going through. In fact, the first time Mary touched my upper thigh, I exploded right away. I was so embarrassed, but Mary told me, "This is just another learning experience; so let me teach ya how to control yourself better. Start by focusin' your mind on anything except what is really happening. Find yourself a 'happy place' to think about and continue to concentrate on it the whole time."

I closed my eyes to find my happy place was in Wisconsin. The memory of the cottage and the hillside next to it became the place I went to every time I needed to blank out my mind. To help me, I bought a scented air freshener which smelled like fresh green grass to replace the mint one and hung it from my rear-view mirror whenever Mary and I went out. Now I was able to relax even more when I needed to.

We would practice this 'routine' every time Mary and I went out. We became regulars at "The Twilight," a local drive-in movie theater. These techniques Mary taught me soon became very comfortable to me, and I felt my confidence level rise in this area.

After many, many nights of us being together and Mary working on relaxing me, I was able to prolong my own excitement for the whole first movie. One night after a particularly exciting practice session, she remarked, "Someday someone will thank you for being so gentle, kind, and for taking your time."

As usual, I had no idea what she talking about.

What I did know was I was enjoying our experimenting. But as I drove home that night I wondered if what I was doing was okay, or if I was doing something morally wrong. I quickly got my answer when I got caught in a driving rain storm.

I knew I couldn't talk Phil into having full out sex with me, but I decided to show him some special moves. I taught him practically everything he knows today, I think. He was a very intense student and not only learned fast, but very well. I showed him how to control his movements to make the girl anticipate and want what was to follow. I got him to relax and to focus on what the girl was feeling, not what he was. As he continued to practice on me, I felt him getting more comfortable with the sexual part of our relationship. After he got better with understanding what a girl wants, we worked on his needs. I taught him how to slow down, relax, and expand his mind so he could last longer. I still don't know why he wouldn't go any further with me, but at least I started him thinking about sex in a good way. I knew someday he would probably be a good, compassionate, and gentle lover. I just hoped I could experience his expertise myself.

After all of this time of thinking sex was wrong and only bad guys wanted it, I added number twelve to my list.

12) **Girls have the same wants and needs as guys. They think about, talk about, and want sex, and are not afraid to show their guy what gives them pleasure.**

Misguided Sensitivity

***

One Friday night I went to pick up Mary and had a beautiful bouquet of flowers with me. I bought her a full dozen red roses, so she would know how I felt about her. When I rang the doorbell her mom answered the door instead. After she asked me in, she saw the roses and said, "Those are beautiful, but do you know what red roses mean?"

"Yes, they mean beauty and love," I answered. "I know your daughter is beautiful and I think I may be fallin' in love with her, that's why I bought 'em."

She seemed impressed, but told me, "You know, I remember what it's like to be young. You may *think* you're in love, but you really aren't. The two of you, especially Mary, are way too young for true love. You'll meet many more girls in your life; so don't push for love, just let it happen. At your age, I think white and yellow roses would be a more sensible choice. Do you know what *they* mean?"

"Yellow ones are for friendship," I smartly answered. "As for the white ones, do you want the traditional meaning or the modern meaning?"

She smiled back and said, "I see you know your roses very well. That means you know the traditional giving of the white rose is a symbol someone is too young for real love. Some girls will push for it, but most aren't ready for it. I prefer the modern meaning—mutual respect and remembrance. To me that has a more innocent connotation. Always remember, though, a white rose can mean many different things, depending on what you want it to."

I thanked her, but had a feeling she was trying to tell me much more than she let on. I thought her talk might be a sign from above to have me re-evaluate my stance on love and dating, so I put all that information in the back of mind for a later date.

***

About three weeks before school was to begin, Mary called me; she was crying. "I need ya to come over right away," she said in between sobs. "I have some bad news."

I drove over to her house as fast as I could. When I arrived Mary was sitting on her front porch, the very same porch where four months ago I got my first kiss from her. Mary hugged me tightly and whispered in my ear, "I'm movin' away. My father is transferring to California."

The first thought which ran through my selfish mind was, *Here's another man who let me down.*

I was always told just before you die your whole life flashes in front of your eyes. Well, that happened to me. Right then everything Mary and I had done together suddenly appeared. It was no wonder that after I blinked, my eyes were filled with tears. I had absolutely no feelings in my body. I slowly sat down with Mary, held her hands in mine, and we sat in complete silence for what seemed like forever.

Finally, I looked at her and said, "Mary, I love you. We can make this work out. Exactly when are ya leaving?"

"I love you, too." Mary cried a bit more and then sighed, "We leave in two weeks cuz we need to get there before school starts."

Two weeks! I felt as if God was punishing me again. He had taken away everyone I let into my heart; Julie, my father, Nana, Jim Croce, Faith, and now, Mary. I couldn't believe the place where I had experienced my best night ever, the front porch, could also be the place where I encountered the most pain. Life sure seemed complicated and unfair to me. As I thought about what happened, I felt a wall beginning to build around my heart. It wasn't a high wall yet, but was there just the same.

I didn't ever want to feel like this again and decided I wouldn't let anyone else into my heart ... it hurts too much.

I took it harder than I thought I would when I told Phil I was moving. I had grown to really like him and the way he treated me. He was a good guy that I didn't want to hurt. When he told me the last time he felt this way was when his dad left, I just cried harder. When he said he loved me, even though I didn't, I felt he needed me to say it back to him.

I now knew we were not meant to be "together forever." What we had was wonderful, but it was now over. When I get to California I will begin the process of moving on with my life. I hope, for his sake, Phil is able to do the same. But before I go, I hope he will give me something extra special to remember him by ... the honor of being his first.

The last two weeks of our relationship went by way too fast. We were always together; I tried to fit a lifetime into those two weeks. Every night we'd go to the Twilight and Mary would beg me to have sex with her. I decided I wanted to, but couldn't follow through on those feelings because I thought if we did have sex, it would make separating even more difficult for both of us.

And strangely, I felt that warm surge which sometimes flowed through my heart once again.

***

The night before she left for good, we went to the drive-in again. This time the feelings between us were totally different. There was no sex talk and there was no happiness; there was only crying and feeling sad for each other. We actually sat side by side, holding hands, and watched the movie. It was the first and only movie we both watched all the way through together. The movie was "Grease."

When the movie ended, it felt like my life did, too. We drove back to her house in complete silence. After I parked the car in the dark driveway, we cried together for a very long time. I couldn't take it anymore, so I said, "This has got to stop. Our time together may be over, but our lives aren't. In time, we'll either be together again, or we'll both forget. Whatever will be ... will be."

I wanted to do something to make us feel better. I thought back to Nana and wondered what she'd advise me to do. I took Mary by the hand, walked to the front porch, and said, "Mary, I want you to do somethin' for me. I want you to remember me in a special way. Instead of crying, let's laugh. Please remember me by the song *Sandra Dee* from the movie we just saw? Ya know, the goody-two-shoes who wouldn't have sex until she got married. Then I started to sing:

Look at me; I'm Sandra Dee.
Lousy with virginity
Won't go to bed till I'm legally wed
Remember me, I'm Sandra Dee.

Mary immediately stopped crying and jokingly said, "You are *so* weird." But then she became very serious. "I'll always remember you for what you are, a nice sensitive boy who taught me how to feel good about myself again."

When I gave Mary both a red and a white rose, symbols of my so-called love, I came back with my catch phrase of, "Yes pretty lady, I can help you feel good."

That's how I left Mary. That was an emotional night for me, but I was able to add number thirteen to my growing list.

13) All good things come to an end — try to end them on a high note.

Well, you can't say I didn't try, but we never did have sex together. Our time had come to an end and I was sad. He tried his best to make me smile that last night. I knew he was a different person when I was around him. I hoped he would be able to bounce back. I missed him a lot more than I expected I would the first few months I was gone. A long time after this happened I realized he was the nicest guy I ever dated ... I probably should have stayed in touch with him. He cared about me, he made me feel special, and he was the most honest guy I ever met. Even though we only knew each other about four months, I find my recollections of those times still make me smile.

***

My life continued without Mary in it. I knew I needed to move forward, but felt the tide of emotions starting again. Unfortunately, another event kept me on the ride even longer.

Up until now, my family consisted of my mom, my brother, and my sister. That all changed when my mom began dating Bob. The two of them started to get along better and better and decided to get married. I was happy for my mom because she deserved a normal life with a man, but it sure made my life tougher. I hadn't had a father figure in my life for at least seven years and was very accustomed to it. Now I was getting a step-father and even though for the most part Bob was a kind man, he was still a man. I couldn't help remembering all those nights my mom and her friends talked about how men were. I was afraid my mom was going to get hurt again. Bob never tried to replace my dad, but he did set up some rules I didn't want to follow; like coming home by midnight, and wanting me to go to back to church every Sunday morning. I was just biding my time until I got older and could move away. The two of us never fought, but we really never got along either, basically I tried my best to ignore him.

Once again I spent more and more time in my room, alone with my records. This was when I began listening more to myself and to the others in my life, instead of my mom. I still had a small connection with her, but Bob replaced me, so I felt she didn't need me anymore.

I had become the person I thought I left behind, and the one I didn't want to be; lonely and in need of more confidence.

Chapter 12 — Joyce

Back when I started to date Mary steadily, I quickly found out I needed much more money. I got a job at a local fast-food joint called The Burger Shack, and like most kids my age, I worked mostly nights after school, and on Saturday afternoons. My personality was the same at work as it was in school. I showed up, did my job, and then left. The only time I was different was when Mary came in to visit. I would suddenly become much more vocal and appeared to be the leader. Once Mary moved away, I went back to being my old self; very quiet, rarely smiling, and not interacting with others. Since I didn't have anything else to do, I changed my schedule in order to work more.

There was a black manager named Joyce who saw this change in me and, just like Faith, wanted to help me build on my potential. Joyce sensed something was wrong and decided to have me work only when she did, which also meant working Saturday nights. Since I didn't have Mary to go to the drive-in with anymore, it really didn't matter to me. Joyce believed I could become a good manager, one who the other employees would listen and respond to. The more Joyce and I worked together, not only did my confidence start to come back, but there became an obvious connection which we both felt. She wasn't as friendly to the other kids as she was to me. For whatever the reason, we were brought together.

Joyce was about four years older than I was. She was tall, slim, and very athletic looking, with a short brown afro which always looked perfect. She always wore a silver bracelet on her right wrist and had a colorful rainbow earring in her pierced right ear.

One Saturday night after close, Joyce and I sat in the restaurant lobby, drinking lemonade, and talking about life. She said, "Ya know, in our lives changes happen all the time. Remember God only gives you what He knows you can handle. I know you've had many changes happen to you lately, like your girlfriend moving and your mom getting re-married. So, how ya handlin' all this?"

"Not well at all," I said. "When Mary was around me I felt more important and seemed to get noticed more. Now, without her, I've retreated back into spendin' most of time alone in my room listening to sad love songs." I sighed and explained, "That's why I work so much — it gives me somethin' to do."

"Phil, you're a nice kid who has a lot to offer. I've seen you when you have the confidence you crave, and you're a great person to be around. What you need to do is learn how to make *yourself* feel good. Just cuz things didn't go as you'd hoped doesn't mean it always will be that way." Joyce put her hand on top of mine. "You're different than the rest of the kids workin' here, you're much more mature than they are, and seem to understand so much more than they do. I'd like to help you regain the confidence you need. Whaddaya think?"

When I asked her how this was going to happen, she explained; "I'll let you run the store whenever we work together. The others will see the confidence I have in you and they'll accept you more."

As this plan began to unfold, I was surprised it actually worked. I felt the others listening and responding to me in a way I had never felt before. I became very comfortable around the people at work. I became their leader; the one they came to for help, for advice, and for having fun with. I had Joyce to thank for this.

One Saturday, Joyce came to work and was definitely not being herself. She was very quiet the whole night, didn't respond to any of my jokes, and actually looked like she had been crying before she came to work. I asked if she needed to talk, but she declined. But as I was leaving for the night, Joyce asked me if I was still interested in listening to her.

We sat in the lobby once again, only it was me who started this time. "I can tell somethin' is wrong. You've listened to my problems, so now I'm here for you. Tell me what's happening?"

"Can I share a secret with you?" Joyce forced a small smile in my direction. "Now, if I tell ya, you can't tell anyone else ... promise?"

I swore whatever we talked about would stay between us.

Joyce started telling me the story of her life. "I'm twenty-one and am on my own—have been since I turned eighteen. That's when my father threw me out of the house for being a lesbian. He couldn't accept that of his own daughter. I really thought that was the lowest time in my life. Well, until last night ... I broke up with my girlfriend, Roberta. We'd been together since my dad disowned me. We shared everything, now I'm alone in the world, and really don't like that feeling."

Joyce continued telling me about Roberta, why they broke up, and the feelings she was experiencing and she cried a little. I offered her my shoulder for comfort and even cried with her. But mostly, I did what I did best, just listened.

After she calmed down a bit, I told her I was curious about something; then I asked point-blank, "What's it mean to be a lesbian?"

Joyce somewhat smiled and began to explain her lifestyle. Again, I just sat back and listened. I was very intrigued by her story. When I asked her if it was a choice she made, she replied, "No, this is something you're born with. Just like you may like redheads better than blondes, I like women more than men."

"What's the hardest part of being one?" I inquired.

"The hardest thing," Joyce said, "after the realization and the acceptance that you're different, is the fact you have to lead a double life. In the 'real' world, I have to be very careful about how I act and who I trust. I don't have a lot of confidence around straight people; I think they know my secret and want to expose it. One false move, one wrong choice on my part on who to trust and my whole life can change. I could lose my job, my home, and even more importantly, my dignity. Please show me I made the right choice in sharing this with you."

I gave her my word I would never betray her trust.

I now knew why Joyce and I connected so fast. We were definitely each different; but we truly felt the same way inside. Neither one of us had enough confidence around people. We desperately wanted to trust everyone, but couldn't bring ourselves to do it.

After listening to Joyce talk, I gained even more respect for her. Even though I thought my life was crazy at the time, she still had it much harder. My mind flashed back to Julie and Janet in grade school and I thought how inside we are all the same; we just want to be accepted and to be happy.

***

Joyce and I hung out a lot together while we helped each other forget our ex's. Joyce told me about a place where she felt the most comfortable. "There's an area up in St. Louis catering to the gay and lesbian lifestyle. Most straight people don't even know it exists. It's where we all go just to be ourselves. It's comforting to know I'm not totally alone in this world. I can share my feelings without the risk of saying something wrong. For me, this area is like utopia."

I listened intently and then said, "Wow that sounds great."

Joyce flashed a wry smile at me and said, "How about you comin' with me to the lesbian roller rink on Wednesday night."

"I don't think so," I backed off. "I don't belong there. It feels like I'd be intruding in on your sacred ground or something."

"The other ladies won't mind," Joyce said, "And if anyone does, I'll have a word with them."

So Joyce started taking me to The Pink Rink, her lesbian skating rink. At first I was very nervous, but soon realized these females were just normal women who happened to like *other* women. This element actually made it easier for me. Since I knew none of them would be interested in me, I could concentrate on being myself, improving my skating, bettering my initial interaction with females, and hopefully getting some confidence back.

These episodes with Joyce and her friends just reaffirmed once again that we are all basically the same. It also became my first interaction with women who were of varying backgrounds, cultures, and races; and ones who had different religious beliefs. And soon I began to believe we really could "all get along."

Before meeting Joyce, my choice of music leaned toward soft ballads and hopeful dreams ... the songs of Air Supply, Bread, Jim Croce, and Billy Joel. I always wished I could express myself the way they did; they were able to tell a story in a song which I connected with. Many of these songs were melancholy, which was a direct reflection of my life, very sad and lonely inside. But those feelings began to fade away after I met Joyce and her lesbian friends.

The music these ladies skated to was called Disco. It was the total opposite of what I was listening to. Disco used the beat of the music and the dances associated with it to tell a story. Most of these stories revolved around sex, although most used innuendos as their method of expressing it. Sex was still something I didn't know much about. Just the same, these songs were electric—very upbeat in nature—and made people smile as they enjoyed themselves. The gyrations which evolved from your body while dancing to this music came directly from the heart. The more you relaxed, the more natural your movements became. People could tell things about you by how you danced. Joyce and her friends called it "feelin' the music."

I definitely felt this music and immediately connected with it. I became totally alive; it awoke things in me I never thought about before. Much to my surprise, I found myself extremely more confident when I responded to it. These girls at The Pink Rink noticed something develop in me also, a comfort zone. They taught me the dance steps, the skating routines, and how to decipher the hidden meanings behind the words.

I thanked each of these ladies by giving them a pink rose as a symbol of my appreciation. The spotlight was again shining on me, only this time, of all places, it was in a lesbian skating rink.

***

Joyce was ecstatic I was back to being happy and, more importantly, that her image wasn't tarnished by me showing up with her. She had worked very hard on making an image for herself which was both acceptable and comfortable. At the rink, she wore very loose clothes which made it easy to skate, was always extremely at ease with her sexuality, and wanted people to know who she was. She proudly displayed her sexual choice on the t-shirts she wore. I also learned the colorful rainbow on her right earring was the international sign of gay pride. The statement Joyce proclaimed was she was a lesbian and she was perfectly okay with it.

The better I got to know the other ladies, the more I learned about them, as individuals. A majority of them weren't as comfortable with their sexuality as Joyce was. Some were very young, many were scared, and many even felt alone in the world. Those quiet and sheltered ones were the girls I felt the greatest connection with.

To let them know how I felt toward them, I began to hand out yellow roses to these special women. It was my way of saying "I understand and I care."

I also learned many of these lesbians had masculine nicknames—such as Duke, Spike, or Butch—given to them by their partner. To show their acceptance of me I was given a *feminine* nickname. To those wonderful ladies in that lesbian skating rink in a far-away part of St. Louis, I became known as "Rosie."

***

One night Joyce looked at me—I was still wearing clothes like my colored bell-bottom jeans, my silver shirt, and the leather shoes that Lisa had helped me pick out—and asked if I liked the image I projected. She explained, "Since you like disco so much you should take a stand and let people know it. You need new clothes."

I knew girls felt that what the men they hung out with wore was important to them, so I agreed to let Joyce reinvent my image for me.

Joyce and few of her black girlfriends took me shopping to a store in their part of town which specialized in disco clothes. I had no idea there even was such a place. After we walked in, I said, "Listen, I have no idea what I should wear, what goes with what, or even what I look the best in. We're all good friends, I trust you to help me make the correct statement. I'm puttin' my life into your hands, so please don't let me down."

The ladies scanned me up and down to decide which clothes would fit me the best. What they saw was a five-foot-eleven, skinny white boy looking back at them. Actually I was a growing boy with hair sprouting on my upper chest, a full mustache, and I needed to shave every morning just to stave off a five o'clock shadow on my chin. My hair was now dark brown, shoulder length, and shaggy. I had a slender twenty-nine inch waist with long legs which were slim and toned. As their gazes followed my legs upwards they said they knew a small, tight ass when they saw one, even though they much preferred it on a woman.

In order to better show off these "assets" they had me try on a pair of Angel Flight pants. These pants were polyester, very form-fitting in both the waist and buttocks, and also had small flairs at the bottom of the legs. This would come in handy when I put on my skates.

I was hooked the first time I tried them on. The fit was so comfortable they actually felt like a second skin to me. After I tried on many assorted colors, the ladies came to the conclusion I should only wear the black ones as they showed off my attributes the best.

On the decision regarding shirts, they wanted me to wear ones that would show off my chest hair and my golden tiger pendant. Once again the material of choice was polyester or silk, as I really liked the feel of both of these. Instead of getting the normal busy disco designs, Joyce had me buy only bright colored solid ones. She explained, "These colors go well with the pants, not to mention your shape."

To finish off this look, they bought me small, thin belts which were the same colors as the shirts and socks.

Joyce smiled and said I was coming around just fine, but needed a few more things to totally complete my new look. The first was a new pair of shoes. She picked out a pair of bluish-gray, ankle high boots. These not only felt great, but also kept those three or four inches to my height I was getting accustomed to.

I tried on one of the outfits they picked out in the dressing room and when I looked into the mirror was flabbergasted. I loved this new image and the way it made me feel. When I made my entrance from the dressing room, the lesbian girls all applauded and screamed when they saw the new me. Obviously, they were extremely happy with their choices. Even the guy working behind the counter seemed impressed, enough to ask me out. He put on a serious frown when one of the ladies told him I was straight. I thanked him just the same and said, "If ever I decide to turn gay, you'll be my first phone call."

Joyce was smiling. "Now you look like how the music makes you feel, but I have two more surprises for you. First of all, we believe a real man should always smell good. Since you need a distinctive scent people will recognize as yours, I'm buying you your first bottle of *Musk Oil*."

A few of the ladies expressed their approval of that aroma.

"Second, as soon we leave here we're going to the beauty parlor. I have my guy waitin' to give you a make-over," Joyce said with a tremendous smile on her face. "He'll add volume and shape to your hair while adding blond highlights to lighten it. I promise you'll love it."

Again, the group agreed with her decision.

Thanks to Joyce, and her girlfriends, I was looking my absolute best. However, even though it was apparent I was showing much more confidence on the outside, what I felt on the inside, where it really counted, didn't change all that much. I knew I looked good in my new clothes, and I would feel good while playing the newly christened role of Disco Phil. I just wished some of these wonderful feelings could transfer over to when I was just me.

Misguided Sensitivity

***

That Wednesday night I was the center of attention, unbelievable for a guy in a group of lesbians. I was such a big hit with her friends Joyce invited me to go with them to a disco club, MainStreet, that Friday night. I had never been in a bar before and was still underage (fifteen) so I wasn't sure I could get in, but Joyce assured me there'd be no problem.

Friday night arrived and as I was dressing in my new clothes to play this new part, I wondered where this experience would take me next. I wanted the spotlight back on me for a long time and I was actually beginning to accomplish that, although I felt a lesbian bar wasn't exactly where I wanted it to be at. I had hoped I could be just as popular at school or, at least, around straight girls.

Arriving at Joyce's apartment, she looked me over, smiled her sensitive smile, invited me in, and asked if I wanted a beer. I'd never had one before, so as I swallowed the first slug the taste took me by surprise. It was bitter and had a real bad aftertaste. I didn't understand why most men, or Joyce for that matter, drank this stuff. I didn't want to hurt her feelings, so I gulped it all down.

Upon arriving at MainStreet, Joyce was right; I was allowed to enter with no questions asked. As soon as I walked in, I was completely taken by the uncommon atmosphere. It reminded me of the Pink Rink, but on a much grander scale, this place had much more life flowing from it. And the smells ... there were scents I'd never experienced before. I would soon learn they were a sweet mixture of marijuana, alcohol, and human sweat. It was an enticing scent, one I quickly learned to thoroughly enjoy.

I met some more of Joyce's friends, and they asked if I wanted a drink. "Ya know I really didn't like the Heineken Joyce gave me at her house, what else should I try?"

One of the ladies I knew from the shopping spree volunteered, "How about white wine? It's sweet, smooth, and goes down easy."

It was strange, but the first thought crossing my mind was of my grandmother saying, "Drinking wine brings you closer to God."

After a few rounds, the taste of this drink began to remind me of Nana's sweet lemonade. The only thing missing was the mint.

We all drank, danced, and had a fantastic time that night. As I drove home, I realized I was fully accepted by a new group of people. I began to see how we really could all fit into the real world together. I experienced new things and enjoyed them all because of this group of ladies. And best of all, I was able to believe a little more in myself, and I realized meeting Joyce was the best thing to happen to me in a long time.

The minute I met Phil I knew he was special. He had a different aura about him and a maturity other boys his age didn't. As a lesbian, I have to be careful who I let into my world. But immediately after talking to him, I knew I could trust him to keep my secret.

Just as I knew it would be, he really felt at home with my friends and was accepting of our lifestyle. He wasn't afraid of us like some guys are, and he never treated us differently. And he was quickly accepted by them.

I could tell he was taken in by the disco music he heard, so I helped him experience it more deeply. We became so close that we could talk about anything. He was the closest thing to a boyfriend I ever wanted. I was glad he let me help him discover another side of life, and to help him understand to just enjoy what comes along.

Although I am as gay as I can be, and never even consider about having sex with men, Phil was the one guy I actually thought about doing it with. Unfortunately for him he was as naive about sex as he was about what kind of clothes to wear.

Chapter 13 — Life After Mary

Mary had been gone about a month and even though I was keeping myself busy with Joyce and her friends, I still missed her. We attempted to send letters back and forth, but that quickly fizzled out — mostly on her end. I guess she found it easier than I did to move on. I was experiencing fluctuating swings in my confidence. I was always extremely high when I was around Joyce and her friends, but very low when I was at school, or at home trying to get used to my new step-father. I was, once again, on the ol' emotional roller coaster. I needed someone to talk to, someone who really knew me, and would understand what I was going through. There was a person who fit all this, but I hadn't talked to her since I ran into her back in April. She told me she would always be there for me, so I crossed my fingers and called.

I started out, "Leese, I'm sorry about the carnival night. Running into you took me by surprise. I didn't know how to react and knowing me the way you do, ya know that ignoring things is the way I usually handle pressure. I'm sorry it took me so long to call you, but I need your help."

There was a long pause, and then Lisa gushed, "I knew you'd call." I breathed a sigh of relief as she went on. "That night took me by surprise, too. I just wanted the two of you to be happy, but when I saw you together I second-guessed that decision. I thought you completely forgot about me, and I was jealous. This call means a lot to me. Let's make a promise to never let anyone get in the way of our friendship again."

I agreed and we started talking about us again. I told her, "I've changed a bit since the last time we talked. I met a new friend from work and she's really helpin' me find myself. Ya know, after Mary moved, I felt real down and out, but now Joyce is helpin' me turn that around. Instead of listenin' to those sad, sappy songs I used to, I now like disco. It makes me feel alive. I'm experiencin' things I've never felt before; all those songs are about sex, even though they never come right out and say so, don't ya?"

Lisa laughed, but then got a little bold, "Speaking of which, did you ever have sex with Mary?"

"We had some very heavy petting sessions," I replied, "but we never actually did the deed, so I'm still an official virgin."

Lisa sighed. "I have to say, I really respect you for that. I thought for sure she would've corrupted you." There was a long pause and I could tell Lisa was debating with what she was about to say. Then she let me have it; both barrels. "Ya know she was cheatin' on ya the whole time, don't you? She told me she had urges that you wouldn't help her with, so she was getting' it on the side."

I was feeling betrayed by Mary, not to mention a rush of embarrassment. "What does she mean I couldn't help her? I did everything she asked except the actual act. You know I should—"

"Get over it, man," Lisa cut me off. "Things happen in life you can't control. You were so blind in love with her you would've forgiven her and just continued your relationship anyway. This way with her gone, it's over, no one really got hurt because of it, and now ya get to go on living."

"I still feel like I've been lied to, but you're right, I have to move on. I just hope she didn't do it with anyone I know, that would really suck."

There was a longer than expected silence on the other end of the phone, but then Lisa asked, "So how's life at home?"

"When I'm not hangin' out with Joyce, I'm spendin' more and more time in my room alone, just like before," I told her, "basically just thinking about my life and why certain things happen to me."

"You should write down your feelings," Lisa suggested. "You also need to get out and meet some new people. Learn to roll with whatever comes your way. Let the chips fall where they may. And if you get hurt again ... hey Phil, it's called 'life'!"

I respected Lisa and put her suggestions into action. I began to write down my feelings, and eventually they turned into poetry. I couldn't share them with anyone yet, but they did make me feel better. I also made a commitment to get my sorry self out there and meet people, even though I wasn't sure how or where.

When Phil called me, I knew right away we still had the connection we once had. We were able to talk about everything again, just like we did before he started dating Mary. We both agreed that friends should always be there for each other no matter what.

I couldn't believe he didn't have sex with Mary; I'd never known her not to bed any guy she set her sights on. Mary wasn't really the one for him after all, but he had to learn that on his own. She was cheating on him the whole time, but he was too naive to notice. He thought he was in love, but for her, Phil was just a conquest.

I knew what had really happened, but could never let Phil know that, whatever story Billy had told him, Billy and Mary were actually an item on the sly. She told me that many nights after Phil left, Billy was right there to help her with those urges she had.

To forget her, I told him to go out and experience the world and all the other girls in it ... how was I to know just how well he would follow through?

Chapter 14 — Gerri, Crystal, Pam, Colette, et al.

I decided to put Lisa's sage advice about meeting people quickly to the test and school would be the proving ground. But I needed some help there, so I started hanging around Billy more often. Billy had become extremely well-liked by almost all the girls, so I was sure he could help me meet some new and interesting ones. Billy was a cool friend, although I always felt as though he was keeping a secret from me, but I never pressed him on it.

I quickly learned he had developed a totally different attitude than I had. I found out he lived and died sex. He apparently had his own mission in life: to meet as many girls as he could to have sex with. This led to some difficult times for me since the girls he set me up with thought I was just like him. Obviously I wasn't. I only wanted to connect emotionally with them and have them trust me. I figured sex would get in the way, or change my thought process totally.

My reputation became the "sensitive sidekick" to Billy. Many of these girls he set me up with quickly learned I would rather listen to them, and try to be of help, than make out with them. I wanted to be friends not lovers, and I just wanted to understand them, not use them.

Gerri was a year younger than I was, yet she was much taller. Being over six feet, she was clumsy and awkward, and most boys steered clear of her. But I always tried to see what a person had to offer on the inside and I wanted to become friends with her.

I attended a basketball game with Billy and his date, and was introduced to her before the game started. We watched the first half in total silence so I had no confidence she was interested in me at all. When the half ended, Billy and her friend left to have sex in the back of his car, which left Gerri and me alone.

I finally worked up the nerve to speak, "Ya know, I like Billy as a person, but I really don't understand him. All he wants to do is have sex. I think that shows a complete lack of respect for the girl he's with. Besides, I was told back when I was younger it's against all God stands for. I guess by bein' a virgin, I just don't get it."

"You're still a virgin?" Gerri looked at me in disbelief. "I used to be until I quickly realized the only way most guys will give you the time of day is if they can get into your pants. It isn't all that bad once ya get used to it, and I've found out when you do it with someone ya care about, it's even better. At least, being the girl, I get to control who I sleep with."

I tried to explain myself further to Gerri, but she suddenly stopped me. "Let's get outta here. I'm here to feel good. Do you at least know how to kiss?"

The first thing which came to my mind was the phrase I often used with Mary, so I jokingly said, "Yes pretty lady, I can help you feel good."

Once we got into the car and started to make out, I had to stop. "Gerri, please don't get mad, but I'm not into this right now. You're a great girl, and I'd love to be friends with you. I feel as though you're just doin' this to get me to like you, but I already do because of who you are, not what you do."

Gerri looked at me as if startled. "You know Phil, I like your style. You're honest about how you feel, you have strong opinions, and ya stand up for 'em. I really respect that. So okay, let's be just friends."

Gerri and I did indeed become good friends. Our relationship was strictly platonic and the subject of sex never came up again, although we many times discussed God and our very different beliefs.

Gerri introduced me to her friends, Chris and Janice. They were both big fans of the soccer team and already knew of me. So after some small talk, I was able to become friends with both of them.

Chris became another girl who I could easily open up to. We would meet about once a week and just chat about life and our beliefs as we walked from the school yard to the famous popcorn store downtown called The Wee Little Popcorn Store. This tiny store was frequented by all the kids of our town, not only for all the great aromas which poured out of it, but for the rows and rows of penny candy that lined the long shelves along its skinny walls. You see, the store was about one hundred feet deep and only about ten feet wide. Since only a few people could enter at a time, all the students hung out in front of it after school, so it became *the* place to see and be seen.

At first I just listened to Chris, but the more we met the easier it became for me to let my true feelings emerge. In fact, Chris became my second "Lisa" when Lisa was preoccupied. She was also the first person, male or female, I shared my poetry with. I took a risk in showing it to her, and when she didn't laugh at or think less of me, I felt some confidence build inside. Chris helped me get this, my first poem, published in a religious magazine where her uncle was an editor.

> What would you say to a guy
> Who knows nothing about you,
> Yet says he's in love with you?
> Not the love which everyone thinks of,
> But a love where caring rules.
> Where nothing except care and help are revealed.
> A love between two people where one of them
> Cares more for the other than for himself?
> A love which, by helping the other person survive

Makes living worthwhile for him?
A love where he hurts when you hurt,
A love where he feels what you feel,
The love which I want with you.
What would you say to a guy
Who thinks all this, but can hardly
Talk to you face to face?
A guy who can admit he's scared
To let his emotions go
For fear of rejection and loneliness,
But knows in his heart that
No matter what, he can't live without you?
Would you say that he is crazy?
Or would you just call it loneliness?
Just what would you say?
What would you say to a guy
Who says, if he could love you,
For any length of time,
Regardless of the consequences,
That I would?

After reading my poem, Janice and I also became close. She once told me, "It takes a confident guy to express himself like that. I understand the meaning behind your poem—love is scary, but somethin' ya want *and* need to experience. I think it may have a hidden meaning though. I also feel it can represent the love you want to experience with God. I sometimes feel the same way."

I never thought about it that way, and never intended it to mean that, but as I reread it, it just may have a spiritual meaning, too.

This was the first thing I wrote that someone else had connected to; it reminded me of when Mary said I could do anything I put my mind to.

Janice and I also began to meet once a week—in the corner of the library to share books, more of my poems, and our religious thoughts with each other. We had drastically different opinions about God and how to worship, but we agreed to disagree. Janice was a small, shy girl who never seemed to have time for a steady boyfriend. She never even showed an interest in pursuing it; Janice was much more interested in religion and the hidden meanings behind things. But after meeting with me weekly for a few months and defending why she didn't want to date, Janice suddenly changed. She finally met someone, right there in the library, with whom she shared many common interests. When they started dating more regularly, our little talks suddenly stopped. I was a little upset at first, but then I liked to think it was because I used the gift I had to help her feel good about herself that enabled her to meet this special person. And in due time I was able to feel a warm sensation flow through my heart again.

***

There was yet another time I felt as though people were "sent" to you when you need them, or when they need you as if by some otherworldly guidance. It came to me the day I met Crystal.

I was swimming at the Southside Park pool one sweltering summer day. It had many baseball fields, a lake for fishing and was where we ice skated in the winter.

Crystal was clearly younger than I, and I thought we had absolutely nothing in common except for knowing how to swim. She first approached me while I was climbing out of the large pool and politely asked, "Aren't you that guy from school who had his poem published?"

When I blushed and said yes, she added, "Janice told me about you … said ya might be able to help me with a problem I have?"

We sat down on the edge of the pool, our feet dangling in the water, and I let her tell me her story.

"I'm pretty insecure about who I am," she opened with. "I can't seem to trust any boy I meet cuz I don't know if they like me for who I am, or for *what* I have."

It was only then I noticed Crystal was much further developed than other girls her age.

"Most guys just wanna date me cuz of my big breasts. They don't really care about me at all. They just want the other boys to see they're with me so they can make up stories about what we've done." I couldn't tell if it was perspiration or tears that glistened on her cheeks as she continued. "I've never done anything like what they say, but that doesn't stop the stupid boys from lyin' about me. It's so unfair … I've got a reputation, totally undeserved, that prevents me from meetin' the kind of boys I wanna date. I'm confused and frustrated by this."

I knew there was no quick fix to her problem, so I did my best to ease her mind. "I can understand the dilemma you're in and wish there was somethin' more I can do other than just listen to ya. But I've learned that sometimes in life you may get burned, but by experiencin' the small hurt that may come from this you can possibly be able to spot the next jerk who just wants the same thing. Always remember, God never gives you more than you can handle. I'm sure you'll come through this just fine, somethin' will happen to make this more comfortable. Until then, just sit back and try to enjoy the attention. There are many girls in our school who would die for any attention from boys for any reason at all."

Misguided Sensitivity

Crystal smiled at this and seemed to relax. We swam together the rest of the day and I made it a priority not to allow my eyes to drift to her bikini top; I kept my eyes fixated on her eyes the whole day. While we continued talking I eventually knew I had made her feel special in a very different way than the other boys she knew.

When we finished swimming, I asked if she needed a ride home, and she eagerly accepted my offer.

On the way, she cheerfully said, "I really enjoyed today. I feel as though we've made some type of connection. You're exactly what I needed." She then put on a serious face. "I love that you're interested in me as a person, not just in my body. You're a decent guy, Phil."

I took a chance, without really thinking, when I asked, "I know I'm older than you are, and that we just met today, but how'd ya like to go out with me tonight?"

I was ecstatic when she said yes, but kept my cool.

Crystal and I decided to go to The Wee Little Popcorn Store first and then to the drive-in that night. She looked very nice, and even comfortable, when I picked her up. She was wearing a red halter top, a pair of tight black shorts, and had on plastic flip-flops. I noticed she smelled of lavender and found that relaxed me almost as much as the scent of mint did.

There were a gang of guys hanging out at the popcorn store as we started to walk in. One of them made a crude remark about how Crystal was dressed, suggesting she looked like a cheap hooker. The rest of them laughed as I confronted the one who made the comment, who was just about my size.

"You shouldn't talk bad about people that ya don't know," I said.

"Shut up," he spat back. "She should be with me, not you. I can pay her much more." He took out a wad of dollar bills and waved them in the air. "How much for a peek at those hidden treasures ya got there?" he called out to her.

Crystal started to cry as she turned and walked back to the car alone. I grabbed the stack of money from his hand, tore all the bills in half; gave him his chance to do something about it, and when he didn't I followed Crystal to the car.

"I'll get you for that, ya bastard," he yelled at me from afar.

Just as I suspected—all mouth, no muscle to back it up.

"Don't let him get to you," I tried to soothe Crystal. "He's just one of those jerks we talked about before."

After we pulled into the theater, I made a conscious effort to keep the trust I earned earlier at the pool. So while we talked before the movie started, I again kept my eyes on hers.

When the movie began Crystal asked if she could move closer to me.

After she did, she took my hand into hers and said, "I want'cha to know just how much I appreciate what ya did for me at the popcorn store. Thanks for standin' up for me. I feel like I can trust you with anything."

With that said Crystal moved her face closer to mine and started to kiss me. I didn't stop her, but didn't encourage her either. She pulled back and asked me, "Is this okay with you? If it is, I really want ya to kiss me back so I can thank you for being so nice to me."

I was getting aroused by now, so I kissed her like I used to kiss Mary. She started to squirm in her seat. When she stopped after a minute, I thought I had done something wrong and started to apologize. But Crystal put a finger to my lips and said, "I'd like you to be the first boy I let touch my naked breasts."

"That's not necessary," I quickly responded. "You don't have to do this just to have me as a friend. I already like you."

Crystal made a hard face. "I know, but I'm in charge now so I demand ya do what I say." She then smiled and said, "I want this to feel good, so just shut up and do it."

I jokingly saluted her and said, "Yes pretty lady, I can help you feel good."

And like a good soldier, I followed her orders. I started to caress and fondle her breasts the way Mary had taught me to. Crystal carefully slipped out of her top and asked me to kiss her breasts and nipples. I followed her directions to a tee, but stopped after a few minutes. When I said we shouldn't go any further, Crystal slowly got dressed, smiled, and then thanked me. She seemed very pleased with herself *and* with what we had just shared together. The two of us cuddled through the rest of the movie in a comforting silence.

On the way home, Crystal shyly asked, "Please don't tell anyone what happened tonight. I'm not ashamed, it was wonderful, but I don't want it getting around school. Please prove to me that I can trust you."

"I promise I'll never tell anyone. What real friends do with each other should stay between those friends," I responded. "You have my word."

She kissed me and told me I made her feel special. Once again, I began to feel that warm sensation flow through my heart.

Although we shared a nice time together that day I never really talked to Crystal again.

Back in high school, meeting Phil was a turning point in my life. He helped me realize I was indeed special and that I had a lot more to offer than just what the boys saw. He was sensitive, but not at all what I was looking for in a boy. I really didn't have anything in common with him, anyway, and decided that even though he helped me with this problem, I didn't want to see him again. A few times he tried to talk to me at school, but I blew him off. Thanks to Phil, though, I

Misguided Sensitivity

became much more open about my sexuality ... and my body. And all the guys who saw my Playmate centerfold spread will agree.

***

With Joyce's help, the confidence I had at work made it easier for me to talk to girls. Pam was one of those ladies. She was a co-worker of mine who was about my height and weight. She had long brown hair which was always messed up due her constantly wearing a St. Louis Cardinals hat. Although she wasn't exactly pretty, she still had a way about her. She was two years older than I was, and had jokingly asked me out a few times while I was dating Mary. When she heard Mary moved, she asked me for real. And this time I said sure.

"I've always liked you," she told me. "You're different than the other guys I know. You seem to listen, you seem to care, and besides, I like your ass."

I quickly learned Pam was a sex addict, a drug addict, and a cat lover which, ironically, turned out to be the worst of the three. Our dates always ended up the same way, at her place. She would have to spray air freshener since the six cats made the apartment smell so bad; then she'd offer me marijuana as she tried to have sex with me. After a few weeks of me saying no, she gave up.

This was the first time the lessons I learned had somehow served me wrong. I must have missed something when I met Pam, because normally I could tell a lot about a girl just by looking at them. Even though this didn't work out the way I wanted, I decided to take the same advice I gave to Crystal; just be happy that someone is paying attention to you.

***

After the Pam debacle I became more careful about who I talked to. Tish was a shy, quiet girl who worked many of the same nights I did. I came to notice she had a distinctive smile which made her whole face light up whenever she flashed it. The problem was she never flashed it enough. It seemed to me she had an issue with how she looked. She was about five-feet-two and had beautiful blonde hair; with freckles on the end of her nose and under her eyes. Tish reminded me of an older version of Jenna from grade school.

One night after close, I asked if she wanted to go to Round the Clock for a cup of coffee and a chat. I was pleasantly surprised when she actually accepted.

She wanted to drive, obviously to be in control, so I let her. On our short trip to the restaurant we listened to what I thought was classical music. It was a cello or some other string instrument. I wasn't a cello type of guy, but this music emitted a certain passion and emotion. The odd music seemed to talk directly to me, just like the lyrics of a Jim Croce or a disco song did.

When we got to the restaurant, Tish started to talk. "I'm the only child of a Navy veteran, so we moved every few months and I've never had enough time to make any solid friendships. We relocated here about six months ago when my dad retired, so I know we're not going anywhere else soon. Joyce suggested I should get to know you better."

Tish took a long sip of coffee, like she was trying to think of something else to say. "I'm glad you talked to me first cuz I never would've taken the first step. Your soft eyes send a comforting message to me. I feel relaxed and somewhat safe."

I blushed and thanked her.

Tish changed the subject. "Since I never had time for friends, I started playin' the cello. It relaxes me, and gives me the confidence I need to get through on my own."

And that's when it dawned on me. "That was you we were listenin' to on the way over here? Wow that music actually talked to me. You have a real talent there. It's a shame you didn't have enough time to make friends, they're really missing somethin' special."

I saw her flash her special smile and felt real good about it. Tish and I shared a few hours together that night and when we parted I felt I had become a true friend, perhaps her first.

***

One night Tish came to work and was extremely quiet. When I asked what was wrong, she said, "I'm real nervous about this Saturday. I have an important recital that will determine whether I have what it takes to enroll at The Pacard's Music Academy, it's very prestigious and I really want to get in. And to make matters worse, the same exact day is also my birthday."

"Take a deep breath. You have absolutely nothin' to worry about," I assured her. "You'll knock their socks off, you're great and ya know it. So, tell me, whaddaya want for your birthday?"

Tish smiled. "Just two little things; I wanna play the best music I've ever played, and I'd really like some flowers. My grandfather always bought me ruby red roses on my birthday, which made me feel special. But since he died, I feel like no one really cares anymore."

So I decided to attend her recital. That Saturday morning, I first stopped at the local florist, Amlings, to buy eleven yellow roses and one

Misguided Sensitivity

red one.

When I got to the musical event, I sat alone in the back row by myself in order to listen to Tish. As soon as she started playing, I realized she had nothing to worry about. Her raw talent, unbridled passion, and deepest emotions came streaming through. The audience applauded the loudest for her performance when she was finished.

I exited the building in order to wait outside for her. She finally came out and was surrounded by her family. That made me a little nervous, but I finally worked my way up to her, handed her the bouquet of roses, and said with exuberance, "Great job, you were wonderful! By the way, Happy Birthday. These are for you. The yellow ones are from me just for being my friend and the red one is from your grandfather. He still loves you, ya know."

Can you imagine my shock when Tish took the roses, but then quickly ran away? I didn't know if she was mad at me, or was just embarrassed, or what? I didn't mean to hurt her ... quite the opposite.

That's when her mom walked up, put her arm around me, apologized, and said, "That was really sweet. I'm glad you're her friend."

I was still in shock. I'd done everything I'd learned. I listened to Tish, I remembered what she said, I became her friend, and I tried to make her day special. I wondered why she reacted the way she did. I never, ever imagined my lessons could hurt any girl.

***

Tish quit her job right after this happened and I thought it was because of me. I felt real bad until her mom came to my work one day with a letter from Tish. I thanked her, then sat down in a booth, opened the envelope and read the handwritten letter.

Dear Phil,

I couldn't believe it when you showed up at my recital, and when you gave me the beautiful roses I was astonished that you remembered. That was so sweet of you, trying to make me feel special. I got nervous and ran away because there was finally someone, other than my grandfather, who deeply cared about me. I was scared of the fact that I didn't know how to handle that a boy could actually like me. While it made me very happy for a minute, I immediately thought about losing my musical talent if I were to get too involved--too emotional. I have a small problem, I keep all my feelings bottled up inside of me and only let them out when I play the cello. I know you could never understand this, but I'd rather be unhappy and continue to have my music, than be happy and lose my gift. Thank you for our talks together, I'll never forget them.

All my best,
Tish.

Tish would never know, but I totally understood what she was saying and exactly how she felt. Still it cut deep she didn't want me in her life.

***

Colette was the total opposite of Tish; she was a big girl, very loud and obnoxious. She had greasy black hair and her face was full of acne. She made a negative impression just by walking through a door.

Colette was hired to take Tish's place. One night at work, she seductively said to me, "I can still remember the first time we met. The way ya said hi, and the way your big brown eyes looked soulfully into mine. You're the kind of guy I wanna go out with, and eventually marry."

I wasn't too sure about this, but still wanted to be friends, so I let that comment pass.

The more Colette and I talked, the more I realized she was actually a very nice girl. She did have some intense emotional issues regarding her size and her appearance, which I sensed made her feel just like the rest of us teenagers—lonely and afraid. She was using her brash loudness to mask her true feelings about herself, just like I used Disco Phil to hide my lack of confidence.

I treated Colette as I would anyone else, or so I thought. One night we were both invited to a party and went together as friends. Colette was extremely happy to be going with me. I never thought about whom I was going with or how the others would perceive us. While walking into the apartment, we were announced by the hostess of the party as boyfriend and girlfriend, but I quickly rebuffed that statement, saying we were just good friends and I was available. The minute those words came out of my mouth, I saw Colette change. She lost her smile and stomped off.

I immediately knew I had made a mistake. I found Colette and said, "Look, I'm sorry. I didn't mean to hurt your feelings, but I wanted everyone to know we were just friends."

"Would it be so awful if I *was* your girlfriend?" she said angrily.

I shook my head. "No, you're a wonderful girl, but most people don't know you like I do. I guess I'm bein' a hypocrite since even though I look at what people have to offer from their insides, I sometimes let people assess me by what they see on the outside."

Colette started to preach at me. "You're not really a hypocrite; you just care too much about what others think. You wanna be accepted by everyone, and that just isn't possible."

Colette paused to let her opinions sink into my thick self-centered head. Then she continued, "Ya know, I don't think you'll ever be able to make an important decision on your own cuz you'll always wonder how it was taken. Others are gonna dictate what you believe is right and wrong and I really don't think you're strong enough to stand your own ground."

That was totally opposite of what anyone else had ever said to me.

She took another long breath and then added, "I also think you'll never stay with one girl cuz you're afraid of missin' the next best thing that might come into your life. Thanks for ruinin' my night."

To emphasize her disappointment, Colette found another ride home.

After I climbed into bed that night, I examined the situation again. I never wanted to hurt Colette; I just wanted the truth to come out. But, was I really being her friend for the right reason? Did what I learned from my lessons mean nothing to me? Did I care about Colette, or about what others thought of me more? Was the pressure of making a good impression more important to me than the feelings of the one I was with? Was I just being selfish? Was making decisions in my life really dependent on what others thought, instead of what I felt? Could I ever trust my feelings to be my guide again?

I knew I tried to treat everyone the same way, but finally realized what other people thought, or wanted from me, could override my good judgment.

Which way would my journey go? Would I actually be able to stand on my own two feet and continue to believe in my own opinions? Or, would I continue to let others decide my future for me?

***

The girls I'd met after Mary were making me observe my life from a new perspective. All of them were extremely different in personality and needs, but were basically all the same inside. These girls reinforced for me the underlying meanings of the special lessons I learned so far; we all want to be happy and accepted for who we are.

I also saw, probably for the first time, not everything is as cut and dried as I thought it should be. I learned you can do the right things and sometimes get punished for it, just as easily as you can do the wrong things and sometimes be rewarded. I realized you can't trust all girls, just like they can't trust all boys.

Each of us has our own reasons for doing what we do, sometimes we understand them, and sometimes we don't. And even if *you* understand them, others may not. All of us have obstacles and fears we must overcome in order to grow. I heard Joyce's voice saying back to me; *God only gives you what He knows you can handle.*

Perhaps the most important thing I had to come to grips with was that sex was a much bigger item than I ever imagined. Both boys and girls thought about it, wanted it, and obviously some seriously needed to have it.

Chapter 15 — Carmen

I was keeping busy, but still not feeling good enough about myself to jump back into the dating world again. My beliefs about wanting to abstain from sex seemed to always take girls by surprise, so I figured it was better to be alone in my room or with Joyce at the gay clubs. This was how Carmen came into my life.

She was a lesbian friend of Joyce and we met one night at the club, Main Street. Carmen was Puerto Rican; skinny, about five-foot-five, long silky black hair, dark almost blackish eyes that mesmerized you, long well-manicured fingernails, and was addicted to gold. She wore gold necklaces, gold bracelets, gold earrings, and even had gold rings on every finger. That color of jewelry complemented very well her cocoa-colored skin. She was always oozing femininity and didn't look like your typical lesbian at all. That night, Carmen also had a flower in her hair; I quickly noticed it was a red silk rose.

Joyce and I were busy dancing when Carmen scooted over and introduced herself. She looked me up and down, smacked her ruby red lips and said, "Joyce was right, you *are* one hot straight guy. If *I* was straight, you would definitely be first on my list."

Alas, she wasn't, so all she wanted from me was a dance.

Carmen had moves I'd never seen before; it was as though she was hearing a totally different rhythm than I was. I tried very hard to keep up with her, but only got frustrated, so I excused myself and walked outside to cool down. Carmen followed right behind me.

She started talking to me with her Rosie Perez sounding voice, "You, my straight friend, are a great dancer for being a guy. You really seem to hear the beats and let your body respond to them. All girls love a guy who can dance. You truly must be a lover, not a fighter."

I replied with a sly smile, "If I was a real lover, why would I be *here*?" She smiled back, getting my joke.

I pointed out, "You seem to move to a quicker beat—do ya hear the music differently than I do?"

Carmen laughed, "The music of my country is much more about bumpin' and humpin' than the American disco music you listen to. My music is the language of love, and dancing is the mating call of our culture. There's much more touching involved because touching is the foreplay to what will follow."

She looked deep into my eyes with her sexy black ones and told me, "You, my friend, have all the moves. I can tell by the way you dance *and* the way you control the floor that you're good in bed. My eyes never lie."

I laughed at her and replied, "This time they did, I'm still a virgin."

"What a waste of sexual energy," she shook her head. "You straight people just floor me."

While we walked back to the dance area, I asked Carmen to help me feel her music the way she did. She readily agreed and then disappeared to talk to the DJ and request some Latin music.

The music started and Carmen put my hands on her hips. She said, "Step one, just follow the beats of my hips." As her body began to sway to and fro, I began to experience it, slowly at first. Her beats were much quicker than I was used to, but I caught on quickly. Carmen smiled at me and mouthed, "Step two." She moved in very close to me and began to shake her shoulders back and forth. The result of this was that her beautifully shaped breasts started hitting me in the chest. I stepped back to avoid them but she stepped in closer. This time she grabbed my hips and made me stay where I was. I got the message; this was part of the dance.

I began to feel her rhythm better and she tightly grabbed my ass with both of her hands when I felt her long fingernails gently pinch me. She whispered into my ear, "You touching me is a part of this, too, ya know, so grab my ass like I have yours and hold on tight." Obviously she was in command, so I did what I was told as we continued to gyrate to the music.

Even though Carmen was a lesbian, I was getting excited, what with the music, the motions, and my pelvis stuck to hers. She was able to feel my hard penis rub against up her and exclaimed, "Yes, straight boy, you have learned this lesson well. Based on what I'm feelin' through your pants, I was right when I said that you'd be good in bed."

Carmen knew I was a virgin, and I knew she was gay, so I said with a hint of sarcasm, "Yes pretty lady, I can help you feel good."

We danced through the night. Carmen and I touched more and more of each other and I got to know the contour of her body very well. By the end of the night I was soaked in sweat. The smell of my Musk oil and her body perspiration became totally entwined as one.

Carmen moved real close to my neck and sexily said, "Do ya smell that? That, my straight friend, is the sweet aroma of sex, pure and simple. My body liquids combined with yours to make our own unique sexual scent. *That* is what dancin' is really all about. It's to make sure you're truly compatible with the one you choose. It doesn't matter if you're straight or gay, man or woman; the way you move on the dance floor will always reveal how good you are in bed. The better your moves, the better your sex is and all girls like guys who can dance."

I put this thought away for another day—dancing is an action girls like. And knowing what Carmen was implying when she said all girls like a man who can dance, I knew I could use that secret later.

With that Carmen reached into her soaking wet hair and handed me her red rose. She said, "This, my friend, is for beauty and love. I know you have both of them hidden away inside, just waiting to get out."

Chapter 16 — Discovering Disco Phil

So I was a hit at the lesbian bars of St. Louis. In my own backyard, I was still just introverted, shy ol' Phil. I wondered how I could be so comfortable in one place and feel so out of place in another. I thought back to the feeling I had when Mary was around me, the one where I thought girls seemed more attracted to me when we were together. I wanted to try an experiment, but needed some help.

I called Billy and explained my idea to him. He readily agreed to go roller skating back at The Roller Wheel with me that weekend. Billy knew nothing of my friendship with Joyce, my escapades at The Pink Rink, or my experiences at the gay bars. He was just excited about the chance to meet new girls.

That Friday night I dressed in my best 'disco clothes' Joyce picked out for me and went to pick Billy up. After he got into the car he laughed at me and asked, "What the hell are you wearing?"

"I've been practicing my skating at a different rink and this is how they dress," I explained. "I feel real comfortable and this is the new me away from school, so get used to it."

Billy just shook his head, and we went ahead with our plan.

When we walked into the rink I was noticed right away. Most of us kids were fifteen or sixteen and wore the typical blue jeans and t-shirts, so I stuck out like a sore thumb. Hearing some crude remarks being made, mainly by the guys, and knowing this would happen, I didn't let them bother me.

I felt what seemed like a hundred sets of eyes watching me as I put my skates on. I already had my own pair of skates, while most of the kids used the gray rentals. Mine were black, to match my pants, and had lighted wheels that glowed as I skated. I felt strangely comfortable as I slipped them on and moved closer to the rink.

When I finally made it the floor, I jumped on and started to skate forward, backwards, and sideways. I was skating circles around everyone else when I heard the buzz build in the building. I knew I made somewhat of an impression, yet no one came near me.

I slowed down and Billy rolled up to me. We exchanged high fives, "What the hell?" He couldn't believe his eyes. "Where have you been? I had no clue you were this good. I'm sure you'll have the girls eatin' out of your hand in no time flat."

Well, that never happened. They all looked, and they all talked amongst themselves, but not one of them approached me. I smiled at everyone and tried to be as friendly as I could be, but it got me nowhere. It stayed that way all night, and the next night, too.

Misguided Sensitivity

On the way home Saturday night, I said to Billy, "Next week I'm gonna bring another friend with me. I want you to watch the reactions of the girls and see if you can hear what they say as they skate by. I'm really feelin' the need to take this experiment up to the next level."

Sunday night I explained my plan to Joyce and she agreed to help me. But then she added, "It sounds to me like you wanna be a playboy. Carmen thinks that role fits ya well. I know what will help."

So Tuesday night Joyce took me to see another friend of hers. This one was a beautician who also specialized in piercing ears. Even though the trend of men having their ears pierced wasn't as prevalent in the late 1970's as it is today, I got my left ear done. Joyce had picked out a golden Playboy Bunny earring to put in the hole. After admiring what she saw, Joyce proclaimed, "Now *everyone* will know exactly what you really want to be."

Friday night Joyce and I walked into The Roller Wheel together. I received the same reception as I did the week before; a few stares, and a few crude comments from the guys. This time I did hear a couple remarks stating at least I was with a girl.

While Joyce and I skated together, Billy followed closely behind us. Halfway through the night, he skated up to me and excitedly reported, "Man, you're not gonna believe this, but you're a hit. I watched these girls skate by you in pairs, they'd talk about your clothes, then your smell, your hair, your earring, and finally how good a skater you are. Man, they think you're hot!!"

Even though they began to notice, they still didn't come up to me like I thought they would. The next night I felt even more girls sneaking a peak at me, but couldn't understand why they didn't approach me.

Toward the end of the night, Joyce went to the DJ and requested the song *Don't Stop the Music* by Yarbrough and Peoples. This was a song Joyce and I skated to every Wednesday night at The Pink Rink. The two of us had come up with a cute little dance routine right in the middle of it and her plan was for us to replicate the dance tonight.

When the music came on, most of the other skaters got off the floor as this was a song they weren't familiar with. As we did our jumps and skated in unison, the edges of the rink began to get crowded as people, especially the girls, strained to see what we'd do next. When it was time for our special dance, the two of us gracefully skated to the middle of the rink and performed it beautifully. After the song ended, most of the girls clapped for us. Joyce gave me a big hug and we both heard the buzz once again take over the rink. People were talking to each other, but still no one came up to me.

Joyce and I discussed this on our way home. "Thanks for helpin' me," I said dejectedly, "but I think my experiment failed. I was hopin' to prove that by havin' a lady by my side that other girls were more apt to approach me. I guess the feeling I had in my gut was wrong."

Joyce thought about it for a minute. "No, your theory is right. Next week I'll show you why."

That next Friday Joyce came with me, but sent me in alone. I nervously walked in, but did get a few girls to wave, smile at me, and say hi.

I quickly changed into my skates and started skating around the rink. Out of the blue, Joyce rolled up next to me. She put her arm around my waist, talked to me about nothing in particular for a few seconds, and then skated off with a sly smile on her face.

I was confused, what was going on? About thirty seconds after Joyce moved on, one of her lesbian friends skated up in her place. She also put her arm around my waist, talked to me for a few seconds, and rolled off smiling. This process continued on for about twenty minutes; a friend of Joyce would skate up, put her arm around my waist, tell me her name and then skate off smiling. I finally understood what was happening. Joyce was using her lesbian friends to help break the straight girls of their reluctance to talk to me by showing them I was indeed approachable.

The trend continued and I became more comfortable and actually started to put my arm around the girl's waist first. Instead of asking their name, I would just say, "Hi, babe!" to each of them. They would blush, smile at me, and move on. Even though I knew they were all shills — and lesbian shills at that, I felt my confidence level sky rocket.

That's when it happened. I was kind of day-dreaming when a girl skated up to me and said, "Hi." I instinctively put my arm around her waist and said, "Hi, babe." When I actually took her in, I realized it was no one I knew. I immediately started to panic, but luckily Joyce skated by just then. When she winked at me, I regained my composure and started confidently talking to this girl. The girl innocently looked at me and rambled, "You're the best skater here. I wasn't gonna come over, but I really like your earring … you're the only guy here with one. I was hopin' you could find time for a couples skate with me later on."

After I said I would find time for her, I finally felt vindicated; my plan actually seemed to work. Skating with this girl who knew nothing about me made feel the best I had yet. But the night wasn't over.

I thought that would be enough for one night, but I was dead wrong. I was skating with this girl when Joyce went to talk with the rink's owner and the DJ about letting me have one special skate by myself that night. She explained, "He's a pretty good skater and every Wednesday night at the Pink Rink he gets to show off to a special number that he really rocks to. Everyone comes back week after week just to see him. Why don't you let him try it here?"

Misguided Sensitivity

The owner watched me skate around and then agreed to it.

Joyce skated over to me and asked, "How ya feelin'?"

I replied, "I'm really feelin' the groove."

"Good, cuz the DJ is gonna play your song and he wants you to do your routine."

I felt the butterflies coming on and my stomach tie up in knots as I started to sweat. Joyce sensed this and assured me, "You always talk about how you miss being in the spotlight. Don't let this opportunity pass you by, just relax and enjoy the moment. My friends and I will be there cheerin' ya on."

I swallowed hard and reluctantly gave her the thumbs up sign.

When the time came for my song, the DJ first cranked down the music and asked everyone to clear the rink. He then announced he had a special guest who was going to give a solo performance. The lights went low and my song came on. I took a long deep breath, closed my eyes in order to remind myself I was just playing a character, and I instantly became Disco Phil. I quickly prayed for acceptance.

The song, by Donna Summer, was called *Hot Stuff*. It was a fast moving disco song, but I started out slowly. I let my inhibitions go and really began to feel the music and became much more confident. Joyce and her lesbian friends moved their way to the edge of the rink and every time I'd pass by them they would try to slap my ass, just as they did at the Pink Rink. Slowly the straight girls started to see what was happening and actually joined in the fun. I was able to totally forget I was in a straight rink, and that some of these girls actually may be interested in me.

There was a part of the song where I made a beeline to the middle of the rink, did a great big jump, and ended with a spin. When I completed this I heard the crowd clapping and whistling. I was on top of the world and felt like my prayers for acceptance were actually being answered this time.

There were a few special lines in the song Joyce and her friends knew by heart. While Donna Summer professed her dreams about sharing her love with a warm blooded lover, they all sang along. By the end of the song, all the straight girls were singing them, too.

Finally my song ended and while everyone was clapping, the DJ shouted over the P.A., "What a performance! Who is that wild man?"

Joyce and her friends all yelled back, "That's Disco Phil!"

I was hot, sweaty, and tired, but I was feeling the adrenaline. Joyce and her fiends hugged me and congratulated me on "making it in the straight world" while other girls I didn't know came up to congratulate me, too. Some wanted to skate with me, and some just wanted my phone number.

When I sat down to relax, Joyce came up to me and said, "Well, you did it. Your theory that girls tend to be attracted to boys who are comfortable with all types of girls is true. We just had to show 'em you were friendly. The more your natural confidence came through, the more this became apparent to them. You really have a great personality, and you'll have a great time here being Disco Phil."

Joyce and her friends had made me what I was. Yes, I was acting, just playing the part of Disco Phil, but I was comfortable with it and I was also accepted because of it. The next issue I had to face was that the real Phil was yet a totally different person than my alter ego. I was still insecure and quiet, and hoping against hope to be a better man. I wished by being accepted as Disco Phil, this would let me show some of these girls the real me behind the character. In the meantime, I would use Disco Phil as my outlet to meet new girls. I felt I could do it. I didn't know what was next, but had I known, I'm sure I would have doubted I was ready.

That night at the skating rink probably was the most fun any of my friends or I had with a guy, especially a straight one. It was such a joy watching Phil's transformation. He was fun, he was alive, and he was himself ... well, okay, he was Disco Phil. He played the part perfectly. He seemed happier than I had ever seen him before. I was glad I was part of making him feel that way. He was always concerned with making others feel good, now it was his time.

I didn't know what was down the road for Phil, but I was sure he would have fun finding out. The one thing I did think about was how this would change him.

He had some concrete thoughts on how he wanted to live his life and the decisions he needed to make. He had strong beliefs, but also really wanted to please others. What others thought about him always affected the decisions he made. With all the attention he was receiving on this night from the straight girls, I hoped ... okay, I knew that sex had to follow. And I hoped he would make the right choices.

Chapter 17 — Star

I became more of a regular at The Roller Wheel and most of the kids began to accept me, especially the girls. I was able to relax and bring small pieces of the real me to the forefront. But I always maintained the part of Disco Phil, which let me become friendlier with everyone so I was finally able to initiate conversations with the girls I wanted to talk to.

My reputation soon came to be known as the nice, sensitive guy you could talk to. It wasn't out of the ordinary for me to spend a whole night at the rink sitting on the sidelines listening to a girl as she complained about her life, her boyfriend, or her parents. I'd talk to every girl who needed me to listen, not just the good looking ones. Most of the guys thought I was weird, some thought I was gay, and thus not a competitor of theirs; but the girls knew better. I continued to go out of my way to help make the girls feel special and a secret was born between "my girls" and me. I hoped Nana would have been proud.

Late one night as Billy and I were skating around the rink, a girl skated up between us. She was very average looking, and seemed to have something important on her mind as she said, "Hi Billy. Hey, do ya mind if I talk to Disco Phil alone for a minute?"

Billy was getting used to this line, so he skated off.

She continued, "My name is Star and I've been watchin' you since day one. I knew you were different than the other guys the minute I saw you walk in dressed the way you were — and you continue to prove that fact every time I see you. The way ya treat the girls here, whether they're pretty or not, really is a turn on. But do you think I'm one of the pretty ones?"

Because *all* girls were pretty to me in one way or another, I replied, "Sure, of course you are."

Star asked me to skate with her the rest of the night.

During the next song, she remarked, "I've seen a big change in you since that first night. Ya came in lookin' all nervous and unsure of yourself, but now you seem to be in total control — not only of yourself, but of all the others. We all can see how you take command of the room with your presence. You also have an aura the color of love. However, I've noticed ya never leave here with a girl. You either go with Billy or quietly disappear by yourself. Does that Playboy earring you wear really mean that you're gay?"

Two things went through my mind. The first was here was another girl who knew about auras. The second thing was this girl seemed to be in tune with what was happening around her. I immediately felt a connection. I was ready to let her experience the *real* Phil that was hiding behind my alter ego.

I asked if she wanted to get something to eat and find out for herself if I liked guys or girls.

I noticed Phil the first time he walked in the door. He was totally different than any other guy at the rink. At first he was shy, but as he met more people he developed this certain confident air about him. I don't think he was aware of this, but all of us girls were. He didn't seem to be scared of anything after the first month. He even had the confidence to dress different, wear an earring, and he wore cologne. None of the other boys did that. Those tight black pants he wore really made his butt stand out. He was dreamy. He was as sexy as any teenage boy could be. Even though his reputation was being "Mr. Sensitive," what turned me on the most was his body. I made up my mind that first day I was going to get him to like me, and some day I would have sex with him. A lot of the guys think he's as gay as a jay bird, but I know jealousy when I hear it.

Star and I went to a nearby restaurant to talk. After we sat down I made a point to listen closely.

"I'm from New Jersey," Star began, "and have lived here for a few months. I'm fourteen, extremely smart for my age, enjoy skating, and seem to be popular among the guys at the rink."

I continued to listen but was also sizing Star up. She wasn't classically pretty — actually she was a little overweight. And she wore thick glasses; normally a turn-off for boys. Her hair was dirty blonde with strands of dark brown running through it; cut short around her face, and feathered back. This wasn't the typical kind of girl a guy would go for. I wondered why she was so darn popular with the boys at the rink.

After talking for a while, I drove Star back to the rink. I held her door open, and as Star exited my car, she reached for my hand; so we walked in holding hands. When her friends came up to us, she boldly announced to everyone we were going out next weekend. I was a little surprised, since I never asked her out. When her friends left, Star apologized. "Sorry about the date thing, but I wanted the other girls to be jealous."

I smiled at her and said, "Since you already have this all planned out, who am I to change it? What's our special date?"

She said she loved the drive-in movies, so we agreed to go there next Friday night.

Nana had told me to watch out for signs and make the correct choices, so I should've seen what was happening, but I was too blinded by happiness at the prospect of a date with a popular girl from the rink; and I was too excited to even think about what might happen next. I was just glad that *something* would.

Misguided Sensitivity

***

Friday night I picked Star up and we proceeded to a new drive-in, the Dirty Thirties. It was called this because it was on old Route 30 and most times showed dirty "B" movies.

When we arrived, I sat back and gazed into Star's large, innocent eyes as she told me, "Phil, you have the gentlest eyes I've ever seen. Looking into them relaxes me and allows me to share things with you that I can't share with others. You're so easy to talk to."

I innocently blushed. All I could say was, "Thanks."

The sun went down and the movie started. Without warning, Star slid over close to me. I recalled this was the fourth time she had taken the lead in doing something. First she approached me at the rink, and then she grabbed my hand before we saw her friends, she basically asked me out, and now she'd moved closer without asking. I was getting the idea she was a little pushy and always got what she wanted.

She gently took my arm and placed it around her shoulder in order to bring her face closer to mine. And then she kissed me. I was taken by surprise and pulled back.

"What's wrong?" Star said, unruffled by my reaction.

"I just wasn't expectin' that tonight," I said, trying to recover.

"Why do ya think we're at a drive-in movie theater?"

"I assumed to watch the movie."

"No silly," Star giggled, "we're here to make out."

"Don't ya think we're rushin' things a bit?" I suggested. "We really don't know each other that well and I don't think God wants me to do this right now."

Star laughed. "Now's not exactly the time to talk about religion. Just sit back, relax, and follow my lead."

Star started to French kiss me and at first I didn't respond. But then slowly I began to feel differently and soon I found myself kissing her the way I kissed Mary many times before.

This time when she pulled back, Star looked me directly in the eyes and said, "I knew ya knew what you were doing. I don't know who taught ya how to kiss, but they did a great job. This is gonna be a fun night for both of us."

So much for her eyes being innocent.

We went back to making out and I became more and more relaxed. I continued using the familiar routine Mary and I practiced so often. I could tell Star was enjoying herself, so when she stopped to take off her top and asked me to use my tongue on her breasts, I didn't need any coaching. She clearly liked what we were doing and I knew I was only giving her what she so readily wanted, so I concluded it couldn't have been all that wrong.

Star started to rub me through my pants as I continued to touch and probe about her body. About thirty minutes into this Star stopped and said, "My hand hurts, why are you still so hard?"

I smiled and explained, "I've conditioned myself to last long enough for the girl I'm with to be able to enjoy the moment more than I do. I'm really more concerned about what you're feeling. This time was for you and you alone, my needs can wait."

Star looked puzzled and said, "You sure are different. I've never had someone care as much about my wants as you."

I suggested we get dressed so we could watch the movie and cuddle the rest of the night.

I was ready to have sex with Phil that night and was very surprised when we didn't. Phil was very good at finding all my erogenous zones. He knew of areas that other boys I made out with didn't have a clue about. He was a gentle and caring person who also was very honest about himself and what he was feeling. He actually cared about my feelings. Wow! And I couldn't believe he could control himself for so long. That is going to come in handy later on. I can tell I am getting closer to having him — next week for sure ... I hope.

Star and I went out again the following Friday. This time when I picked her up I couldn't ignore what she was wearing even if I wanted to. She had on an ultra-thin blue tank top, and clearly had no bra on underneath it; plus a very, very short dark blue mini skirt. After she slid next to me, she seductively whispered in my ear, "I'm not wearin' any panties." Just before she kissed me, she gave me the most devious smile I'd ever seen. Then she told me, "This is your lucky night."

I asked her why and she answered, without missing a beat, "Because tonight I'm gonna let you fuck me!"

Anxiety hit me right between the eyes. This was the part I knew nothing about. I was either scared — thought it needed to be saved for someone extra-special — or something I couldn't articulate.

I couldn't say exactly why I didn't want to experience sex, only that I knew I didn't. I also realized I couldn't tell Star I was a virgin, for fear of what she would think. This was the ultimate test from above. My mind raced back to church, those sermons about heaven and hell, and God's expectations of us. Would this be acceptable or would I go straight to hell? I fell back on what I was good at — I tried to ignore the whole thing.

It was already dark when we pulled into the Dirty Thirties and found a place to park. Star took control, as usual, and as soon as the car stopped I had literally seconds to decide whether to tell her I was a virgin and stopping this nonsense, or having to "go with the flow" and give her what she wanted. I realized there was no way I could bring myself to tell her I was a virgin, so reluctantly I decided to let Star run the show. This just confirmed for me what Colette insisted to be true: *Other people will be making decisions for you your whole life.*

Star was in complete control as she undressed us both and then helped us maneuver in the bench seat so everything was easier. After a short, few minutes of intense kissing, she wasted no time in grabbing my penis and helped me enter her. On the radio, *Just the Two of Us,* by Grover Washington was playing so I started to move to the rhythm of the music I was listening to. To me I was dancing, just horizontally.

It was a nice slow song, so I too went nice and slow. When the song ended, we were still in the middle of what we were doing. More songs started, and finished, and we were still going at it. I continued to think only about the music, my happy place, and about Star. Luckily being inside my car, I smelled the scent of the fresh green grass air freshener lingering in the background and that made me relax even more. We continued making out and I didn't stop to think about me, about what was actually happening, or worse yet what may happen next.

***

Afterward, as we dressed, Star said, "Man, you're one of a kind."

I didn't really hear her and never acknowledged what she said because I was feeling things I had never felt before. My mind was running wild. I thought about Mary and the special things she taught me. I thought about Carmen and what she said about me being good in bed. I also revisited my thoughts about caving in to pressure and what Colette said about me not being able to make decisions on my own. I then wondered what tomorrow would bring; and I prayed real hard I wasn't going straight to hell.

What I didn't think about was the warm feeling I sometimes got in my heart, because for some confounding reason it wasn't present at all.

***

On the way home, Star told me, "You're an exceptional lover. I'm pretty experienced, but no one has ever made me feel the way you did tonight. You must've done this a million times before. You were so slow and in control."

I couldn't lie to her, so I said, "Thanks for the compliments, but I need to tell ya tonight was my first time. I never ever wanted something like this to happen to me until I was married. I have to say it was nice, but bein' my first time, I have nothin' to compare it to."

"You're way too honest. Where have you been hiding?" Star gave me a kiss, and said, "So, how's losin' your virginity make ya feel?"

Again I just ignored her, although I figured I had a smile on my face a mile long, since I could feel it.

She added, "Don't look at it as an ending to something; it's just the beginning of new things."

In record time my mind turned 180 degrees and I found myself second-guessing if what I had just done was wrong in the eyes of God. I didn't want to believe in a Deity who severely punished people for their indiscretions, but I really didn't have anything else rock solid to put my faith in. As my thoughts continued to torture me, a slow mist started hitting my windshield.

I had a plan for that night; I wasn't going home until we had sex. I put on my hottest outfit and really played it up hot and heavy when Phil picked me up. I told him right up front he was getting lucky. I wanted to see if he could last as long as he said he could. Well, he put every guy before him to shame. I had to ask him to stop after I had two orgasms because I was getting tired. That was the first time I got to finish before the guy did. He was never thinking about himself. It was the best overall experience I ever had, and I could not believe it when he told me I was his first.

He touched me in places I didn't know existed—but I know I taught him some new things, too. He was a decent guy who really cared for the girl he was with, but I knew the day would come when I would need to move on, it was just a matter of time.

Star and I had a few more dates and always ended up at the Dirty Thirties, where I added what she taught me to the routine Mary and I had perfected earlier. *Now I knew why she was so popular with the boys at the rink.*

One of those nights I gave her a red rose and explained, "All roses have hidden meanings, this red one means love. I believe I'm fallin' in love with you."

"No, you're not," Star stopped me. "You may be in love with what we do, but you're not in love with me. We're much too young for that."

"Doesn't making love mean love to you?" I naively asked.

"We never made love," she said firmly, "we had sex. There was no emotional connection, not for me, anyway. I just wanted to have some fun and that's what it's been. Let's not complicate things with talk of love."

I was confused and tried to talk to her about it many nights at the rink, but she would quickly cut me off. I was hurt, but not the hurt I felt when Mary left. I felt more like I had lost a certain part of me.

Misguided Sensitivity

Finally one Friday night, Star got angry. "Look, you don't seem to understand my words too well. We've got a good thing goin' and ya keep tryin' to muck it up with this 'love' business. So here's a message that means we're through." With that she flipped me off, then climbed out of my car and with all her might slammed the door.

She could stop seeing me, but she could never make me forget what we did. I tried to put the whole Star incident out of my mind, but for some reason it wouldn't go away. I realized I finally experienced sex, and whether it was right or wrong, I didn't die because of it. Most important, I actually proved to myself the person who was able to make at least one particular girl feel good, was *the real Phil.*

In the final analysis, I have to admit Star came into my life at just the right time. Because of her, I finally understood sex is fine if you respect the girl you're with, and you must always be honest with them *and* with yourself.

I was happy I was finally able to go through with it, but at the same time I was also sad because I felt like I did it on Star's terms. I wondered if I somehow had let myself down. I wasn't ashamed, I just wasn't sure I wanted to do it again anytime soon.

Chapter 18 — Carmen Returns

I was feeling a little unsure of myself the following Saturday night when I went dancing at MainStreet with Joyce. One minute I was happy I'd experienced sex, the next I'd be questioning if it was really the right thing to do. Even though I felt intensely different inside and thought everyone else could sense what I had done, no one had actually said anything to me about it, not even my mom.

Carmen spotted me from across the room and our eyes met instantly. She motioned for me to join her at her table. As soon as I sat down, she looked right through me with her deep brown eyes. She slowly softened up, smiled seductively at me, and said, "Congratulations, straight boy."

I was confused. "For what?"

After smacking her lips like she always did, Carmen replied, "Your brown eyes just told me that you've had sex. I told ya that you were a lover."

I rolled my eyes at her and asked for an explanation.

Carmen began to teach me something new. "Your eyes are the gateway to your soul. The soul lets off an energy that escapes through them. And just like a person can tell how good you'll be in bed by how well you dance, you can tell if a person is open to the sexual experience by the look in their eyes. Your eyes, my friend, now tell me a totally different story than the last time I saw you."

I was fully unconvinced.

Carmen saw this and said, "Let's do a test to prove what I say is true. Look at the brunette sittin' at the next table. Can you see the brilliant gleam radiating from the corners of her eyes?"

I turned to see a woman who wasn't all that attractive or friendly looking, but I did see a gleam coming through. So I asked what it meant.

"Not so fast," Carmen exclaimed. "Now look at the girl she's with, and tell me what ya see."

I looked at the other lady, who was extremely pretty, and had the most beautiful blue eyes I had ever seen. But as I looked closer, I didn't see any gleam. In fact, all I saw were dull, lifeless eyes staring out at the room.

"All right smart boy," Carmen smiled deviously, "which girl do ya think would be more open about havin' sex with you?"

"The plain-lookin' one with the gleam in her eyes?" I meekly responded.

Carmen slapped me on the knee. "Now straight boy, you have the secret many men don't know about. Enjoy your future! Just don't overuse it, or start usin' it for the wrong reasons."

I laughed and gave her small peck on the cheek. She surprised me by asking for a real kiss.

"I thought you were a lesbian?" I said quizzically.

"I am," Carmen shot back, "but I wanna see what I'm missin', and what makes those on the other team so fascinated."

So I kissed Carmen on the lips and was surprised again when she slipped *her* tongue into my mouth. Not to be outdone, I responded with one of my best French kisses. Carmen pulled away saying something in Spanish which I didn't understand.

She grabbed my hand, took me to the dance floor, and we danced the way we did the first night I met her. We began to move to the beat in perfect unison when her eyes met mine. I could see the gleam she just told me about shining brightly through them, so I playfully said, "I can see your soul and it's tellin' me you're a red hot lover. Why can't you be straight?"

Her eyes stayed glued to mine and Carmen raised her eyebrows, flashed her award-winning smile, and replied, "Even if I was, and even though the way you dance tells me you too are a great lover, I'd still be too much for you to handle."

I smiled back and thought to myself, *I don't doubt it.*

Although I hoped I could use this special talent later in my life, I didn't add it my list. I wanted it to stay a secret not everyone knew about.

Chapter 19 — Cece

I thoroughly enjoyed being around Joyce and her friends. They knew the real me, they accepted who I was, just as I respected them. And because of Joyce, I recovered after the Tish and Colette experiences, so I was as close to being the real Phil as I could be at work.

At school though, it was another story. I continued to feel uncomfortable around the girls, and still had a very difficult time communicating. It was fine when they approached me, but I couldn't initiate anything. Even though I liked school and got good grades, it still wasn't as happy of a time as I had hoped.

Luckily, I had the skating rink to counterbalance how I felt at school. Even though I was still playing the part of Disco Phil, I did allow small bits and pieces of the real Phil to come shining through.

Since Star and I stopped seeing each other I hadn't had sex again. I didn't really think about it and I certainly wasn't looking for it. I felt happier just listening to and occasionally offering advice to the girls I met at the rink.

Wednesday was a slow night, so I was skating around by myself when this red-headed girl skated up to me and said hi. I looked up and was excited to see a girl who was my height, had freckles on her face matching the color of her hair, and had skin so light it was almost transparent. The low pigment of her skin made her green eyes look all that much more brilliant. Right away I noticed the gleam in her eyes Carmen told me about. This girl was lanky, but had a nice figure. She put her arm around my waist and told me her name was Cece.

After a couple of laps, Cece asked if we could sit down and talk. This was normal for me, so I agreed. She said, "I'm here for a reason. I don't normally skate, but it was suggested I come here so you could help me. Star told me about you and how ya made her feel at the drive-in. I'm feelin' down and could use the same kind of lovin' you gave her. Are ya up for it?"

I was surprised at what I heard, not that Star would talk about our intimate experiences. I already knew girls talked to each other about sex and their needs, but I was more surprised Cece had the nerve to ask me point-blank about it.

After I saw what her eyes were saying to me, I figured having sex again would be just fine. I was pretty sure I wouldn't go to hell for doing it a second time.

I was really intrigued by her looks, as I always had a soft-spot for redheads. I said, "I'm glad Star spoke so highly of me. It's too late to go to the Dirty Thirties tonight, when would ya like to go?"

"I have a better place," Cece bluntly replied, "and we can leave right now."

With that she started taking off her skates, so I followed her lead.

Before we left, Cece had to make a phone call so we stopped at the pay phone. I heard her side of the conversation only. "Yes, we'll be there in about ten minutes ... I don't know, just a minute."

Cece asked me, "What kind of car do ya drive?"

I told her, not knowing why that was important.

We got into my car and drove for about ten minutes down the road. We turned into a long, dark, driveway. After we followed this access road to its end, I saw it lead to a parking lot which overlooked the river. This was the very same spot we all saw back when Billy, Lisa, Mary, and I first drove to The Roller Wheel.

There were other cars parked, so I found a place among them. After I turned the Road Runner off, I saw there was a grassy area between the cars and the river bank. There were people of all ages standing around, laughing and joking; and the amber glow of what I assumed were cigarettes lit up the dark.

Cece lit one herself and said, "My friend'll be here in a few minutes, just hang on until then."

I was confused as to who was coming and why, but innocently trusted Cece; so I turned up the radio and just sat back. I then recognized the familiar smell from the bar Joyce took me to and knew the cigarette Cece had just lit up was actually marijuana. When she offered me a puff, I politely declined. I was already pushing my limits with God by experimenting with sex and didn't want to get in any deeper. To my surprise, it didn't seem to bother her.

Cece asked, "What kind of music do you listen to?"

"I really like disco music and the Latin beat, they're both great to dance to." I added, "But at home when I'm alone, I listen to slow love ballads by Bread and Air Supply."

She smiled at me and asked in a sexy voice, "And what about when you're havin' sex?"

I didn't know how to answer since I'd only done it with the faint sounds of a B-movie soundtrack playing in the background. But I thought of a clever answer and said, "Whatever you listen to."

She winked at me and slid a tape into my cassette player. I heard a car approaching, and as I looked into the rear-view mirror I got real nervous as I realized it was a cop car. Cece reassured me by saying it was her friend. When he walked up to my window and asked to see my license, I was more confused than ever. He then wrote something down in a little black book and asked where I wanted my sticker. Cece told him to put it on the back bumper. When he returned, he looked at Cece and gave her the thumbs up approval, then said to me, "Welcome to the club, I'm sure you'll enjoy it."

I had no idea what he meant and Cece knew it. So after basking in a few more moments of my confusion, she started to explain, "This is private property owned by a few friends that are all cops. You've just been invited to become a member of 'The Submarine Watchers Club' by one of them. You can now use this parking lot at any time to do anything. You can smoke pot, drink alcohol, or even have sex. The only caveat is you must use this car—that's what the sticker he put on your back bumper is for. All the kids in town know about this place, but not all of 'em can use it. Now, thanks to me and Star, you can."

With that being said she turned up the cassette player, slid close to me, and whispered in my ear, "Now it's time to show me what ya can do."

Cece took the lead, just as Star had done before her. I started my new routine and just as she helped me enter her, the tape she put in started to play *You and Me Against the World* by Paul Williams.

Cece wrapped her arms around me, closed her eyes, and whispered, "Take it slow and gentle, and treat me like you care."

I quietly responded, "That's the only way I know how to do this."

Cece and I had sex as the tape repeated itself twice. She wasn't as vocal as Star was, so the whole time, I wondered what she was thinking about, which helped me last even longer than when I was with Star.

Cece was kissing my neck when I felt her cheek rub up against mine. I swear I felt tears come down her face a few times, but didn't say anything about it.

While we were getting dressed, Cece said, "Star was right, you are truly special."

I thanked her and then added, "This night was for you, not me. However, I sense there is something wrong. You wanna talk about it?"

Cece sighed, lit another joint, and then replied, "I've had a rough life. The way I forget about it is to have sex. As I do, I block out all the old negative memories and try to get lost in the moment. Unfortunately, I like to get lost a lot."

She took another drag, "Thanks for everything. It's like you were sent from up above. Star said she thinks you need to share your gift more often. And afterward, we think you should give the girl a small token. All us girls like a remembrance, ya know."

Cece then got to the point. "You once gave Star a rose—we talked about it and think you should get some yellow silk roses that you can hand out because most of us girls are just lookin' for a friend who really cares."

Although I was a bit confused by what she was saying, this time the sex made me feel different ... sort of a warm sensation penetrated my being.

Cece handed *me* a pink silk rose when I dropped her off back at the rink. After she left, I sat in the lonely parking lot and thought about what she had said. I was feeling sorry for her, and wondered how she came to be that way. Then I wondered if sex really could make you forget all about everything else.

I thought more about her and Star's comments. Was having sex with someone really *helping* them? Should it be saved for a "one and only?" Or, should it be shared with many?

Unfortunately, I didn't have any answers to those questions. All I knew was I now experienced sex with two girls and they both had no qualms about it. I still wasn't sure if I did yet, but I did like the attention it brought.

I couldn't wait to see Cece at the rink again. I wanted to see if she was indeed happier, but I never got that chance—she never came back.

Because of this, Cece become my first one-night stand. Or should I say, I became one of *her* many one-nighters.

Star told me about Phil at school one day ... the times they had spent together and how good he was. She said he was naive about sex, but was still a natural. He would make me feel like no one else ever did. She knew about my one-nighters and suggested that I give him a try. She also recommended that we get him into the club so other girls could share what she called "his gift." Star was right about him, he was a slow and sensitive lover who only thought of me. He treated me with a respect I didn't deserve and had never gotten before.

I knew I could never go back to the rink for fear of falling for him. Being that he was everything a girl could want, and knowing I couldn't handle that kind of responsibility, instead I just got him into the club and I left, although I do wonder just how much he will use this "free pass" to fun and excitement.

Chapter 20 — Deidre

A few weeks after meeting Cece, Billy and I were skating together and he started talking about all the girls he had sex with. He seemed inordinately proud of the number, and was more than happy to share with me all the details about them.

"Have you been able to partake of any of the girls here since becoming so popular?" he asked as if he was a connoisseur.

I let out a little laugh and said, "I don't do that, although it does seem like they're okay takin' advantage of me."

This concept seemed to stump Billy. After I recanted my stories of Star and Cece, I asked him, "Is sex that important to you?"

He smiled and said, "If I could have it every day, I would."

When I asked him about love, he responded, "What's love got to do with sex? They're two separate things. Don't ever get 'em confused and don't let any girl trap you with the claim 'I think I'm fallin' in love with you.' Most of these girls are too young to know anything about it, and couldn't handle real love if it showed up on their doorstep anyway."

While he was talking, my mind wandered back to Mary's mom and the comment she made about white roses and being too young to understand true love. That thought led me back to what Cece said about friendship and caring. In their own ways, all three of these people had told me basically the same thing.

Later that evening, we noticed, as did every other guy in the place, an older looking girl walk in alone. She was well over six feet tall, had short brunette hair, with a roundish face which was perfectly made up. Her cheeks were pink with rouge, her smallish eyes were highlighted with blue, and her full lips were a bright red in color. We both wondered out loud why she was alone.

She wasn't for long. As soon as she skated onto the floor, every guy went up to her. One by one they came away empty-handed. Billy finally looked at me and said. "Well, I guess it's my turn to try."

He skated in her direction and I sarcastically called out to him, "I hope you have fun with that one."

I watched Billy skate up to this girl and start to talk. She actually smiled at him, so I thought he was making progress. She then said something else to him, which made him look my way and point at me. The next thing I knew, this beautiful tall girl was sitting right next to me.

"My name is Deidre and Cece is a friend of mine."

I immediately asked how Cece was doing, not realizing what she really meant.

Deidre politely said, "Cece is fine, but I'm not. I'm twenty-two and recently broke up with my boyfriend. I'm having a real hard time forgetting him, so Cece suggested I come looking for you."

I was flattered Cece said nice things about me, but I wasn't too sure if I wanted to follow through with this. I excused myself saying I needed to go to the washroom, but I was really buying time to think. Billy saw me and skated in to see what she wanted from me.

When I said, "She wants to know if I'll have sex with her so she can forget her boyfriend," Billy just shook his head and said, "You're so lucky."

I asked him what he'd do if he were me and he quickly answered, "No question about it, I'd sleep with her. Whenever a girl asks you that question, you never say no."

Deidre drove me to her apartment without saying a word. It seemed as though she was deep in thought. As we listened to the car radio, I heard jazz for the first time and felt myself relax. When we walked into her apartment, she asked if I wanted a drink, but I declined. She poured herself a glass of red wine and very quickly drank it down. She came back through the kitchen door and hit a switch that turned the stereo on. The cassette which played was by Bobby Caldwell. Deidre told me she always listened to him when she was depressed.

When she took me by the hand to lead me to her bedroom I noticed she had taken control, just like the other two girls. This time, though, things seemed to be rushed. I thought maybe she was having some second thoughts, so I asked, "Is everything alright? You seem to wanna get this over very fast, are you sure you wanna do this?"

Deidre looked at me with a twinge of guilt in her eyes. "I really need to, but I just can't get my old boyfriend out of my mind."

I thought back to Mary and remembered her trick to get me to focus more and said, "Take a deep breath, close your eyes, and now picture whatever makes you happy. As this picture comes to you, continue to concentrate on it. Just relax, and let whatever happens happen."

I then kissed Deidre. The longer I did, the more she began to respond. I went very slow and deliberate. My mission that night was to make this last as long as I could so she'd enjoy it thoroughly.

I was in the middle of my new routine when I felt Deidre finally begin to relax. It started with her breathing easier and then continued when her body loosened up. She opened her eyes wide, smiled at me, and said, "Thanks, now I'm in the mood."

I continued to make my way down her body with my tongue and stopped at her belly button. That's when she pleaded, "Don't stop there, please go all the way."

"What?"

She laughed at me and said, "I guess maybe I can teach you a new trick."

That night Deidre, just like the girls before her, taught me a new twist to my routine.

After listening to her, practicing what she told me, and finally getting the hang of it, I openly admitted, "I really enjoy doin' this. Are you havin' a good time? Do all girls like this?"

Deidre said, "You're very good at it and yes all women like it, whether they admit it or not. It's the ultimate female power trip to have a man down there at their mercy. Women like to be in control you know, and this just confirms they are."

As I moved back down, Bobby Caldwell started singing *What You Won't Do For Love*. Based on Deidre's reaction, I was willing to do this anytime ... for love or whatever.

***

Deidre and I continued to have sex and it was obvious I made her forget her boyfriend for a while. When we were finally finished, I said, "I hope that I was all you expected, and I need to thank you for teaching me somethin' new. I know I'll never forget this night."

She gently looked back at me and said, "Cece told me you were different. She said that you were very honest and had no problem talking about what you just experienced. She told me you were very polite and always put the girls' feelings before yours. You didn't disappoint me and you helped me forget my problems for a while. Cece also told me you are always concerned with how God sees you. Believe me, He's happy or else He wouldn't have given this gift to you."

I blushed, even though I didn't totally understand her.

"I want to thank you for an enjoyable evening. I hope you had as much fun as I did." Deidre then added, "By the way, Cece gave me these to give to you; she says you'll know what to do with them."

She then handed me a big box of silk roses. They were pink, white, red and yellow. On top of these was a note which read, *A different color for a different meaning.* I smiled when I realized none of these fake flowers had thorns attached to them. Thanks to my grandmother I knew all roses had thorns and you needed to be careful when handling them so no one got hurt. Since they didn't have any I figured I didn't have anything to worry about.

There was also a single black rose meant for me. A note attached to it said: *A black rose to signify the farewell to your virginity.* It was signed by Star.

After I gave one of the yellow roses to Deidre, I wondered how Cece knew I would agree to her plan ... and what I had just started.

Misguided Sensitivity

***

On the way home, this time it was me who sat in silence, although my mind was racing. I was just barely sixteen years old, learning and doing things I never thought I would. These three girls I've had sex with began to reshape my thought patterns regarding who I was and what I did. All of them appeared to enjoy what we did together and were even willing to show me new things.

Though they all seemed happy with the outcomes, I was getting a little confused. Only twice I felt a warm sensation in my heart, as if I had done something to help someone. Why didn't I get it all the time? And what exactly was this feeling, anyway?

I had no way to know if what I was doing was right or wrong. I had been assured by the girls it was fine with God, and He hadn't killed me or sent me to hell yet, so I figured it must have been all right.

I also had no way of knowing the lessons I learned earlier would lead to this. I only wanted to have the girls like me, but was this the way to accomplish it? Was this my way of showing someone I cared for them? Or was I just doing this because *they* wanted me to and I couldn't say no?

Once again, I had no answers. What I did know was one of the lessons on my list: *girls have wants and needs,* seemed to ring perfectly true. And after my latest experience with Deidre, I was able to add another lesson to my list.

14) Be open to learning new things and trying new experiences.

Chapter 21 — Too many to name ...

I didn't know what to think after these three girls came into, and just as suddenly, dropped out of my life. The more I thought about it, I was able to conclude they entered into my life just when they needed to. All three were looking for someone to help them through a rough time and, for whatever reason, I guessed God had chosen me.

I truly realized how much girls talk to each other, as more and more young ladies began approaching me at the rink asking if I would share what they called "my gift" with them. Since only three girls knew the origination of this saying, and only one continued to skate, it was a safe bet Star had to be the one behind my sudden surge of popularity. Because of this I was able to take another step in my incredible journey, possibly one that wasn't such a good idea, and definitely one I wasn't too sure I could understand. I liked the attention this brought to me, but did I like the outcomes?

A few things came to mind — one was I thought it was odd all these new girls were coming to me and asking about sex. Luckily enough for me, I never had to initiate anything. But becoming selfish, and believing their tales of me being able to help them in a different way than just listening, I actually began to believe this *was* a gift and that it did indeed need to be shared. The whole time my intentions were nothing but honorable.

My belief became: *As long as I was giving the girls something they wanted and they were perfectly okay about there being no commitment, it surely couldn't be wrong.*

So every Friday a new girl would come up to me and ask the same question, "Can ya help me feel good?"

My pat answer became, "Yes pretty lady, I can help."

I would then be accompanied by someone new to the private parking lot and would share some time with them. Sometimes we talked, but most times we shared sex. Then, afterward, I would always get the same response. "You're so sensitive. You took your time, you cared about me — as a person, and you put my feelings ahead of yours. Thank you."

The one thing all of these girls who sought me out had in common was they obviously weren't looking for a committed relationship. So I assumed each one was probably a one-night thing, and wanting to end it on a high note, I would always reply, "No, *thank you* for allowing me to make you feel good." Then I would hand them a yellow silk rose which stood for friendship and caring.

Although I was happy to be "of service," I was confused that after we had sex many of the girls wanted nothing more from me. There had to be

Misguided Sensitivity

a reason why, but I guess it wasn't the time for me to know yet. That was when I realized Mary's mom and Billy were right, these girls didn't want, and couldn't handle, true love.

The more this happened the I began to believe it was the girls who were playing a game with me. They found someone to give them what they wanted, someone who gave them sex without involving any true feelings, and without either one of us getting hurt. And I was always willing to take care of their wants and needs.

This was when I decided to forget all about God for a while. I stopped wondering if what I was doing was right or wrong, and just did it. And I wondered, Could this be a thorn on those fake flowers I gave out? And could anyone get hurt by this? But I quickly forgot those thoughts.

Clearly the only thing these girls wanted from me was sex. To most guys this may have been a dream come true, but wasn't what I truly wanted. I really longed for a closer relationship with just one person, centered more on the emotional than on sex. I knew I craved connection more than these girls did, but I also felt the timing wasn't right. I would know instantly when that one special person entered into my life.

So until that time arrived, I decided to continue to give the girls the only thing they really wanted from me anyway: good sex with no strings attached. Besides, I had to be honest; you couldn't call what was happening to me "torture."

Instead of yellow roses, I started giving out white ones, which now meant to me the girls involved weren't old enough to understand what real love was.

And I was able to add another lesson to my list:

15) Practice makes perfect.

Chapter 22 — Three lives come together.

I was living three distinct lives; I thought Joyce had it hard.

At The Roller Wheel I was Disco Phil who gave the girls whatever they wanted. I really enjoyed I was able to gratify them all, that they seemed to respect what we did, and basically that they liked me. These girls trusted me. While the way I was achieving this was definitely different than how I anticipated, I still felt my mission of being accepted by females was truly being accomplished.

At The Burger Shack I was still the leader, but in a different way. They knew nothing of my life at the rink. I went to work to listen to and offer advice to those girls who needed it. I was the same ol' guy I used to be at the rink, before all the sex began.

At school I was pretty much just a face in the crowd. I was still extremely quiet, basically keeping to myself; more interested in getting good grades than worrying about what people thought of me. With the rare exception of some of the cheerleaders I had photographed and those who knew me from soccer, I thought most people didn't even know I was alive. So I went to school to disappear, and to think about the secret "other person" I had become.

I was sure there would be a day when all three of these personalities would somehow come together, but I wasn't looking forward to it. I actually liked being a different person at different places, it reminded me of acting. The day they all started to come together arrived much faster than I expected.

I was in a journalism class filled with thirty other students. Our assignment was to research and write an article about a problem which affected our lives. We were told by our teacher, Mr. Dumas, some of us would be asked to share our reports with the class and may have an opportunity to get it published in the local paper. After asking some of the other kids what they were doing their paper on, I was still lost on what I was going to write about. Most of the kids were doing theirs on cancer or some other deadly disease, the energy crisis, or drugs. I didn't want to be doing the same as everyone else; again, I wanted to be different.

That night at work I happened to mention this to Joyce and she came to my rescue again. "Phil, you could give a firsthand account of how divorce affects teenagers. I even have a friend who is a psychologist — she runs a teenage support group and I could ask her to give you an interview."

I was intrigued and after agreeing, I was able to set up a day in order to meet Joyce's friend.

Later that week, I drove to St. Louis and was able to meet with Marcy at a tall skyscraper where she had an office and held all of her sessions. She reminded me of Joyce; she was black, she was tall, and she was a lesbian—so I felt a connection right from the start.

Marcy told me, "Many people don't know how bad this problem is because most people don't like talking about divorce. One out of every ten teenagers are affected by it. Many of those end up blaming themselves for what happened. They tend to retreat into their own little worlds because they don't trust most people and don't want to get close to them. A majority will turn to sex, drugs, or alcohol to suppress their true feelings."

That's when it dawned on me. All the thoughts I'd been feeling had just been confirmed; I wasn't weird and I wasn't alone. My retreating into the world of music like I did, my overwhelming need for acceptance, and my turning to sex was in fact my way of reacting to the divorce.

I wrote the article and began to understand myself better. This didn't mean I was going to change what I was doing, but at least now I had a handle on *why* I was doing what I was.

When Mr. Dumas named me as one of the students who was to read my article to the rest of the class, I became worried. This was school, where I didn't have the confidence level I had in other places. On the day I was to read my article, I stood up in front of my classmates, Mr. Dumas, and the editor of the local paper, and started out very nervously. I closed my eyes in order to visualize both Joyce and Marcy urging me to be natural and honest, but mostly to just be me. I reminded myself this was an opportunity to finally share a slice of my world with a group of my peers (except for the part about sex, of course.) The more I talked, the more in control I became. I started to feel like the day I was a freshman in that senior drama class. I was now on center stage with the spotlight shining brightly on me and I wanted to revel in it.

When I said, "One in every ten teenagers is affected by divorce" I heard a hush come over the room.

"Think about it," I said emphatically as I surveyed the room with my gaze. "There are thirty students in this room, which means at least three of us are affected. Now imagine our whole class—there are over three hundred students, which means that probably thirty of them come from a broken home. Now multiply that by the number of kids in this school and you can see how big an issue this is. Too often these teenagers don't talk about the fact that their parents are divorced, and many of their friends don't even know about it. Most of them will turn to drugs or alcohol or *something else* to help them get through. These people don't interact well with others because they believe they are alone and no one else can help them."

I continued talking and felt everyone listening intently to what I was saying. I was wrapping up my talk when Mr. Dumas interrupted to ask a question. When fifteen hands went up in the air, including mine, after he asked who this affected in the room, they were all astonished.

I quickly added, "It makes absolute sense to me so many in this room are affected. The statistics show that many teenagers who fit this mold throw themselves into an introverted activity, like music, poetry, or writing. This way they can take their feelings and share them without risking the one-on-one contact. I just want you all to know I'm one of those statistics and I'm here for any of you who just want to talk. Remember we're not the problem, but we *can* be part of the solution."

The reaction to my speech resulted in my article being published in the paper. It also became the second thing I wrote which made a connection with someone, or in this case, a lot of "someones."

I felt good about being able to share this information with the other kids and I said a small prayer this superseded anything bad I had done in God's eyes lately. I didn't get anything in the way of a direct answer, but this did lead to many of the other divorced kids, mostly the girls, seeking me out in order to talk. All of these people became *acquaintances* to me. They never became *good friends*, but we shared some nice times together and I felt I was able to help them better understand what they were going through.

Although the guys couldn't have cared less, the girls and I shared a secret. They knew I was there for them and would do anything to help them feel more comfortable about themselves. To these special girls at school I became their sounding board, so I was always listening to someone new and helping them with their problems.

I was now Phil, the divorced kid who cared. And I felt important and wanted; once again I knew Nana would be proud of me.

Chapter 23 — Kayla

Kayla was an extremely nice looking senior girl who had a very hard time associating with the other students. Her parents had been divorced for five years and when she heard my speech, she connected with me immediately.

Upon speaking to her for the first time after class, I saw a five-foot-five beauty with long brown hair and the most amazing brown eyes I'd ever seen. Instead of possessing either the trust sparkle or the sex gleam I normally saw, they shared with me a look of wonderment. Kayla desperately wanted to know how to make friends. Since the divorce of her parents, she had immersed herself solely in art, painting the most incredible landscapes I'd ever seen a kid do. Her beautiful paintings told far better stories than my photos ever could.

Kayla was quiet but very inquisitive, she only wanted some answers, and hoped I could help. The more we talked to each other, the more she opened up. I found out she had lost her faith in God some time ago because of what she had gone through. We started hanging out together—so much that some of the other students thought we were actually dating. This helped her confidence immensely. Not only did Kayla start attending my soccer games, she became involved in making posters which advertised the games, and were then put on the player's lockers.

After a big win, Kayla asked, "Hey, how about you and me going out on a real date? I've never been on one, and I want to at least once before I graduate. Most people think we're dating anyway."

I was taken by surprise, but accepted.

I got real nervous when she answered my question of what she wanted to do by saying, "I would love to go roller skating."

I quickly thought to myself this may just bring two of my lives crashing together. Dare I risk it? I made my decision, "Kayla, I'd like to take you skating, but first there's somethin' you must know."

I told Kayla all about my reputation at The Roller Wheel. I tried to explain Disco Phil to her the best I could, and only agreed to take her after asking for assurance she wouldn't give my secret away at school. There was trust in the air when Kayla told me, "I'd love to experience your other life ... and I promise to tell no one."

***

I picked Kayla up Friday night and she did a double take when she saw how I was dressed. I was wearing a bright blue polyester shirt with the top two buttons left unbuttoned in order to reveal my tiger pendant and chest hair. I had on my signature black Angel Flight pants held up with a blue belt which matched my shirt perfectly, and my spit-polished gray boots. Plus, my confidence level was totally different than when I was at school.

She recovered and said, "I can't believe you're the same person I know from school. Not only do you act differently, you actually look hot in that outfit. I can see why you're in demand."

When we walked into the rink, she got to see firsthand just how popular I was. Girls came up to me to talk, to flirt, and sometimes to try and get me to leave with them. That made Kayla a little uncomfortable, so she went to sit down for a while. This was the wrong thing to do as she was quickly mobbed by several girls, all asking her questions about me. They especially wanted to know if she would be going to the parking lot with me. Kayla became extremely confused and rattled by the attention, so she waved me over and asked if we could leave.

Once we got to the safety of my car, she began to grill me, "How do you put up with that every week? What was that parking lot thing they all were talking about?"

"There are many girls who want me to help them with things. Some need someone just to listen to them, but others want more," I explained. "We all share a secret—the parking lot in question gives us a safe place to do whatever comes natural. I just follow their requests and give 'em whatever they want. We basically just share some guilt-free time together."

Kayla looked relieved and said she wanted to go back inside. This time she welcomed the other girls, asked them some questions, and actually began to enjoy herself. When a few of the girls I had taken to the parking lot started talking to her, I saw her facial expression change. To my amazement, she started smiling, then she was laughing, and she looked very comfortable. I hoped I opened a new side of Kayla that would help her gain more confidence at school.

Well, I must have brought out something in her, because as skating ended she grabbed my arm, put it around her waist, and said excitedly, "Hey Disco Phil, let's go to the parking lot."

At first I couldn't tell if it was innocence I saw in her eyes, or the sex gleam, until she announced, "I've never made out with a boy and I want to see what I'm missing. I want you to be my teacher."

I wasn't sure I wanted to do this with Kayla, but I tentatively agreed.

We got to the river bank, parked, and I went to put in a cassette to listen to. I couldn't find one, so I just turned on the radio. I asked Kayla to slide over close to me and then I started out kissing her very slowly until I really felt her begin to feel comfortable. I was dumbfounded when

Kayla whispered in my ear, "Disco Phil, make my first time something I'll never forget."

This was the first time I was going to be someone's first and it brought back bad memories of *my* first time, along with a quick reminder of what Gerri had once told me, *At least I get to pick the guys I sleep with*. I couldn't let Kayla feel the same way I did about my first time, especially after she just picked me.

So I tried my best to make Kayla feel comfortable. "Just relax and follow my lead," I said as I felt her heart trembling and her body shaking. But she never second guessed her decision.

We began to have sex when a song came on the radio which made us both stop what we were doing and wonder if somehow this whole thing was planned by something larger than the two of us. The song was *Lean on Me* by Bill Withers.

After we resumed, Kayla whispered breathlessly, "I've never felt like this before. I can't believe I was scared of this happening to me. I'm feeling so alive."

I told her to close her eyes and put those memories away for a rainy day.

Afterward, we were cuddling and Kayla said, "I'm so glad that you were the one who I could share this with. You were so gentle, so in tune with what I needed. You've helped me feel alive again."

I thanked her for the compliment and presented her with two silk roses; a yellow one, so she knew I was her friend, and a white one, to remember this moment forever. This was the first time I gave out a white rose that didn't mean the girl wasn't old enough to understand real love. Mary's mom was right; a white rose *can* mean many things.

Kayla always had a strange way with words and this time was no different. She said, "You're just like a gardener who lovingly tends to his garden, then waits for the results that all his caring will bring. When they arrive, those results become his reward. Tonight I feel like I'm your garden, so I will bring you many rewards in the months to come."

Once again I had absolutely no idea what a girl meant.

Phil was so easy to talk to, he actually listened to me. We became friends fast and started hanging out together. I think he was surprised when I asked him out. I was astonished to find out about his other personality at the rink. It really fascinated me that he could be an unknown at school, and then be so popular at another place. When the girls started telling me what he did, I knew I wanted to experience that, too. I didn't know if I liked him for him or for what I hoped he would do to me.

After we got to the parking lot everything just fell into place. I felt so alive afterward, thanks to Phil being so careful and sensitive. My friends who hated their first time came to my mind. I knew I couldn't help them, but I wanted to help other girls enjoy their first time. We girls have to stick together you know. I told Disco Phil—or was it the real Phil—that he was special and because of that he would be rewarded; little did he know how.

***

Well there you have it, my two personalities just meshed together. I hoped Kayla wouldn't say anything at school, but knowing girls talk and share, I wasn't holding my breath.

One night as I was driving alone down a dark stretch of a lonely highway, I started thinking about if what I was doing was morally right. I'd been going to the parking lot quite a bit lately, and while in the beginning I was able to feel a kind of warmth inside, I wasn't feeling it at all lately. I actually thought I was leaving a small part of me behind each and every time.

I would go with the purest of intentions; ones of helping a new girl experience whatever she wanted, and I still truly felt like I was helping them all grow. But I knew it wasn't what I anticipated using the lessons for, at least not as I learned them. Yet I still felt as though all the girls did like me.

I had some questions enter my mind. Was I really helping these girls? Was I helping myself? If I felt like I was always leaving a part of me behind, why did I continue to go? What was I getting out of these relationships? Would anyone ever get hurt by this?

I walked through the lessons in my head and came to the conclusion no one could get hurt—including me. I always stuck to my vow: *Don't let anyone else in my heart.* Even if I didn't do it consciously, not one of these girls, not even Kayla, were able to penetrate the armor that shielded my heart.

And for the first time, I truly realized I really had no deep feelings at all for these girls. While I did feel a mixture of something—regret, anxiety, and possibly I was deluding myself I wasn't doing something wrong—*maybe these trysts weren't as guilt-free as I thought.*

Since I had come to expect I'd be having sex with every new girl I met at the rink, it occurred to me maybe I was actually using these girls for something other than offering them 'help.' I had to admit, Carmen had warned me, *Don't use your gift for the wrong reasons.*

I wondered if maybe I was the one who was too young for true love. I thought I might want to change what I was doing, but expectations seemed to precede me.

I pulled over to the side of the deserted roadway to ask for help and forgiveness, and soon felt some light rain come through my open

Misguided Sensitivity

window. After a few minutes of getting wet, I closed the window and smiled to myself when I realized God really did listen to me, even when I didn't get a direct response.

I breathed in the calming fresh grass scent from my air freshener and was able to picture Nana and me dancing together in the warm Wisconsin rain. I got out of the car to bask in the warm water which reminded me God had forgiven me once again ... I hoped.

Getting back into my car, I realized I couldn't share my inner thoughts with any of the girls I already knew, or any other girl from the rink because of their preconceived expectations of me. I needed someone new to talk to, a person who wasn't so involved in my life, someone who knew nothing of what I had become, and especially someone who could help me find the real me again. I clasped my hands together, turned my gaze heavenward, and prayed I could find that person quickly.

Chapter 24 — Stacey

Stacey and I had been working together for a few months, but never really hit it off. I was different, but Stacey was even more out there than me. I was respected at work, but she was considered offbeat. Her hair was bright magenta in color; she wore wild eye makeup, and used the brightest red lipstick I'd ever seen. She was bigger, well chunkier, than most girls, but that didn't stop her from wearing short mini-skirts and tight tops. Stacey never went anywhere without her knee-high, shiny, black leather boots. She never seemed to care what people thought about her, so I figured she was in complete control of her own life. Although her appearance turned some people off, I looked past it.

It was a cold and rainy afternoon when I walked into the break room we all shared only to find Stacey crying. I sat down next to her and said, "Hey, what's wrong?"

She immediately stopped crying and replied defensively, "There's nothin' wrong, I'm just fine."

Normally I might have accepted that answer, but I could tell something was really bothering her. "How about you and me getting some coffee after work today? That way, if ya do wanna talk, I can listen."

Stacey considered my suggestion for a moment, then sadly shook her head yes.

Sitting in a corner booth, away from all the noises and distractions Round The Clock normally had going on, we quietly sipped our coffee. Stacey finally let out a sigh and began. "I just wanna fit in. Because of what I believe in, what I like, and my weight, I have no real friends. I've got a few acquaintances, but they only show up when they want to, not when I need them to. Is it really my fault I happen to like peculiar things?"

It was interesting to me that even though Stacey and I were so different, we felt some of the same things; it reaffirmed my belief we all wanted to be happy and accepted. Besides, I also used the word "acquaintance" a lot and felt most people I knew were only around when they needed something from me, too.

"I totally know what ya mean. Tell me, what are some of these 'strange' things you like?"

Stacey's eyes lit up. "I really like *The Rocky Horror Picture Show*. It's a new movie that has already developed a cult following. The hundreds of people who go see it dress up like the characters, bring props, recite the words back to the screen, and always have a blast doing it."

I'd never heard of this movie, but was intrigued because it seemed so

Misguided Sensitivity

distinctive. When I asked if I could go with her, Stacey smiled. We agreed to go the following Saturday night midnight showing in downtown St. Louis.

When I picked Stacey up, I saw she was indeed in costume as one of the characters. I was feeling extremely out of place when we got to the movie and I saw almost everyone else had also dressed up. These "regulars" knew what was happening and because I wasn't dressed up, they all knew I was a 'virgin.'

It had been a long time since I was a virgin at anything.

Instead of actually watching the movie, I focused on the audience, their reactions, and all the wild fun they were having. It became an experience I would never forget.

On the way home, Stacey explained why she liked the movie. "The people who go to 'Rocky' are all in tune with themselves. All of us have two sides, the one we show and the one we try to hide. The movie gives us a common bond, and by acting out a character we can relate to, it allows our hidden side to come to life."

What she was saying made sense to me. In a weird way, I was living that same experience as Disco Phil. "Can I come along again?"

"Only if you dress up!" Stacey enthused. "Which character do you relate to—and why do ya wanna let that side out?"

"I wanna go as Doctor Frank-N-Furter," I replied quickly. "I can see he is confused about who he really is and wants to find out the truth about himself. I feel that way all the time. I may not be a transvestite, but I can still feel his pain."

Stacey nodded. "And beside that, your legs and ass will look very cute in fishnet stockings."

***

Stace and I became weekend pals and attended the movie as often as we could. She always went as Magenta, the maid of Frank. Magenta was real easy to dress like. Stace would tease her red hair, the actual color of Magenta's in the movie, so that it would stand on end. She wore a white maid's cap and apron, and under the apron she had a dark black underwire bra with blue, red and purple sequins. She wore a knee-length black dress that had buttons all the way down the front so as she opened the top ones you could see the bra and as you opened the bottom ones you could see her black panties. She added black stockings held up by a plain black garter belt and always wore spike heeled, mid-calf black, granny boots. She looked as hot as an over-sexed maid could look.

I, on the other hand, had my work cut out for me. Stace had to help get my outfit together and we actually used Joyce to help. Joyce and her friends knew of this movie, so she wanted to join Stace and me every weekend. The thought of having her by my side again made me even more confident I could pull this off.

Frank had black curly hair so first we had to find a wig. Every week Stacey would then make up my face, since he wore blue makeup and eye liner. I wore a black sequined corset, laced up the front and with thin shoulder straps, complemented by seamed fishnet stockings, black satin undies, and finally black open-toed platform sandals with white heels. To accessorize, I needed a black garter belt, some oversized pearls to wear around my neck, and black half-finger, elbow-length gloves with silver threads. Finally I added a 3-row rhinestone anklet. We got extremely lucky and found all of this at a costume store in Joyce's neighborhood. When I put it all together, I really looked the part and actually liked how the outfit made me feel. Since I was always very comfortable playing someone else, I became great at being Frank-N-Furter.

The three of us spent more time together so Joyce eventually told Stacey about her sexual preference. Like me, Stacey also became a trusted cohort. Neither Stacey nor I were gay, but we always accepted people for who they were.

We were sharing confidences with each other on night when Joyce excitedly told Stace the part about turning me into the persona she called D.P at the rink. Until then, Stacey knew nothing of that "hidden" side of me, but now it was out and Stacey decided she wanted to experience it in person. We all agreed we would go skating at The Roller Wheel the next Friday night so Stace could see Disco Phil in action.

That night I wore a silver metallic shirt and a brand new shiny black pair of Angel Flight pants with a silver belt. After polishing up my tiger pendant, I added a black cowboy hat for effect. I looked into the mirror and hoped Stacey would like what she saw.

I first picked up Joyce, and then headed toward Stace's place.

When she hopped into the car she said, "You look fabulous. The outfit really fits you. Is this Disco Phil or just plain old Phil?"

"When I'm around you I'm just regular old Phil, but the girls at the rink want Disco Phil, so Disco Phil's what they're going to get."

Once the three of us started skating, the usual things began happening. Girls of all ages started to gravitate toward me, asked for a skate, or blatantly asked me to take them to the parking lot. Neither Stacey nor Joyce knew about the parking lot yet, but were going to find out quickly. Some of the girls I had been with in the past surrounded Stacey and eagerly explained our secret.

When we got into the car for the ride home, Stace started the conversation by asking, "What is this I hear about a parking lot and some secret you and the girls have?"

Misguided Sensitivity

At first I was taken back, but quickly realized the girls from the rink were of course going to tell her all about me. "An acquaintance of mine set me up in this club which allows me to use a parking lot overlooking the river for whatever 'recreation' I see fit. I mainly use it to have sex with the girls who ask me to. That's the secret," I explained. "I give them exactly what they want, and since it makes 'em feel good, I figure it can't be wrong."

"What? It sounds like you're just using those girls?" Joyce said, clearly unhappy with me.

Then she hit me with, "What about your relationship with God? How do ya think He feels about this? I remember when you shared with me the special lessons you learned and how they were supposed to make you feel liked and respected. Is this what they've come to mean to you?"

"I'm not using anyone," I argued. "If anyone is, it's the girls who are using me. Besides the sex, I listen to their problems and concerns. I *am* being respected and liked, and that's what the lessons are for." I hit the steering wheel with my fist for emphasis. "I've always believed God's message is to treat each other with respect, to be sensitive to the needs of others, and to be there when someone needs you. So, in *your* mind, maybe I'm goin' about things totally different than you expected, but in *mine* that's all I'm doing."

"You know, he's right," Stacey weighed in. "If he's just givin' them what they want, how is he to blame? I really think he is helping these girls—so it doesn't look like a problem to me."

Joyce became quiet and didn't say another word until I dropped her off at her apartment. That's when, as she forcibly slammed my rear car door shut, she abruptly said, "Goodnight!"

As soon as Joyce left the car, Stace slid next to me. I saw the sex gleam radiating from her eyes when she asked, "Would you ever consider taking me to this parking lot and letting me experience your secret?"

Before I could answer she put her hand on mine. "I have a lot of respect for you and what you do for these girls. I totally understand what they're goin' through."

Minute tears began to form in Stacey's eyes. "You sensed I was lonely and tried to help. You went with me to the movies, even dressed like a transvestite, and eventually became my friend. All the while you were helping me deal with my feelings of insecurity, and finally you made me realize being me was just fine. The girls at the rink told tell me about how terrific you make them feel. I've never experienced anything like that. Would like you to show me how?"

I felt as though she was reaching out, yet here I was faced with a decision that revolved around sex again. I tried to explain, "Stace, I don't seem to connect the same with the girls I take to the parking lot as I have with you. I don't wanna lose that feeling."

"I promise that will never go away," Stace said softly. "Wouldn't sex be better for you if you actually cared about the person? Think about how nice it would be if both the girl *and* you felt good about what you just shared?"

For a split second, Gerri popped into my mind as I remembered her admonition: *Sex is better when you actually care for the person.*

All the while we drove to the parking lot I was debating with myself whether this was right or wrong. As we pulled in, I was still keeping my options open. After parking I slowly started to kiss Stacey and within a few minutes found myself more aroused than ever before.

This time the physical act was the same, but my feelings afterward were totally different. Even though I didn't allow Stace to enter my heart, I actually felt more of a connection with her than ever before. What I experienced that night made me realize Gerri was correct. Stacey confirmed it when she smiled and said, "They were right, you know; you *do* have a way of making us feel special."

For the first time in many, many months, I became aware of the warmth pulsating through my heart again. At the same time, I also began feeling as though I was once again alive.

Stacey was right, after that night nothing changed between us, we stayed friends, still went to the movies, and we shared sex more often. We helped each other feel good when we were down. I realized sex could be a fantastic part of my life, when I actually felt something in return.

Phil surprised me when I met him. He was open, he accepted others at their inner value, and he tried so hard to help them feel okay about themselves. He always told me he had no confidence in himself, but by the things he did and how he was able to carry himself, I could tell he really was very confident and actually liked himself; unfortunately he just wasn't aware of it yet.

That night at The Roller Wheel I found out way more about Phil than Joyce did. I talked to the girls while she skated with Phil most of the night. All the girls at the skating rink adored him—he thought for the sex—but it was really all about how he treated them. What he saw as unfeeling one-night stands was actually the girls' way of sharing his unique talent of making them feel so special with each other. This was their secret. They never told him that, but ....

His sensitive side had a way of making you feel as if you were the only one in the room. He said he had a fake caring for these girls, but I knew that he actually cared for each and every one of us in his own special way. He really understood how the girls felt.

The sex was just an extra bonus for all of us.

***

Misguided Sensitivity

Before Stacey, my life had become like a bad black and white photograph, dull and lifeless with no feelings at all. With all the meaningless sex I was experiencing, and all the practically nameless, faceless girls coming in and out of my life, I felt as though I was just going through the motions. The perceptions of dire emptiness in my gut, and the bitter loneliness I sometimes felt afterward, reminded me of Julie's book about trusting your feelings. She gave it to me when I was in grade school, and made me realize I should have trusted mine long ago.

That roller coaster of emotions I used to be on had turned into a slow carousel ride that just continued going round and round. In my life, there were no more high highs or low lows and, in many ways, I missed those feelings.

After meeting Stacey, my whole attitude for life began to change. It was like I fell asleep in Kansas and woke up in Oz. The colors were brighter, the music sounded better, and my mind immediately became crystal clear.

By finally having sex with someone I actually cared for, I enjoyed the experience that much more. Stacey reawakened what I had lost—the one thing all men judge their life by—the feeling of accomplishment.

***

My mind wandered back to my early teachings of religion and my belief it didn't matter how or where you worshiped God, as long as you did. The experiences I was having at the rink made me believe that *it* had become my own little church. And in a weird way, I had my own little flock of believers.

To me, religion always meant seeing the difference in people, treating them with respect and sensitivity, and then making them feel good. I truly believed that was exactly what I was doing every Friday and Saturday night. If there really was a God, and if He was looking down on me, I thought the best I had to offer came shining through while at the rink and at the drive-ins. I justified I was doing exactly what He asked of us: spreading the word of love. I just did it literally, and horizontally.

It did pass through my mind that maybe the warmth I felt in my heart could sometimes be a sign from God that what I was doing was right after all. But, I quickly let go of that absurd thought as I realized the God I knew would never approve of what I was doing. And I wondered if I did.

***

It had happened. The two separate and independent lives I was living finally came together and I had some new tough decisions to make. Which person was I going to be? I really liked the half of being Disco Phil and wanted to be more like him, but I thoroughly enjoyed, and needed, the quiet half of being the real Phil. I finally decided to try to merge them together in order to become one whole person.

Because of my relationships with Joyce, her friends, and now Stacey, who all knew and liked the real me, I felt I had gained confidence in all areas of my life now. I began to relax more and just let things happen. I made a promise to myself I would continue using the lessons I learned in much the same way. I would continue to be different and sensitive. I would try to listen to, and enjoy people by seeing what they had inside, not only by their outward appearance.

I focused even more on seeing the differences in all people and accepting them for who they were. I decided age didn't matter to me. I promised myself to be there for whoever I felt a connection with, or felt like I could help.

Even though I still mostly wanted to see the sparkle of trust develop in a girl's eye, I decided when I experienced the sex gleam radiating from them, I would follow through on that, too. So unfortunately, against my true feelings, just like Cece before me, sex was soon to become my way of healing all the ills … in both the girls' lives and my own.

Chapter 25 — Kayla Returns

Even though my two personalities had come together, I still felt different at my three main hangouts. My confidence level was always the highest while at the rink. This allowed me to become very comfortable approaching girls, actually looking them in the eyes, and asking them to share some time together. Every Friday night after skating I would take a new girl to the parking lot in order to share our secret and then present them a white silk rose.

These synthetic roses I passed out changed their meaning in my mind, now symbolizing a loss of the girls' innocence. Even though the girls still thought it was a way for them to remember our shared times, I knew the real meaning and sometimes it would hurt me.

I also began handing out more pink roses because I truly wanted to thank many of the girls for what they gave to me. Since I desperately needed some *real* friends, I gave out yellow ones to those who really meant something to me.

Some of the girls began wearing these in their hair the following weeks while skating so the silk roses became a status symbol at the rink, which eventually led to even more and more encounters. And because of the girls wearing these night after night, I always had a constant reminder of who was who, and how they made me feel on the special night we were together… *Another secret between me and "my girls."*

Before leaving The Roller Wheel each Friday, I would make a date with someone new and take them to the Dirty Thirties on Saturday night. I continued to feel I was being sensitive to their needs, and while I still felt respected, the memory of Joyce saying I was "using the girls" lingered in my mind.

***

At work, my confidence level was rising. After hanging with Stacey, the other girls at work saw me in a different light and they started to ask me out more. And, by using what Carmen taught me about looking for the gleam in a girl's eyes, I was able to pick out the girls I wanted to take to the Dirty Thirties on *Sunday* nights.

***

In school, my confidence level was getting higher because I was using my listening skills with the girls. I was sharing a different secret with the girls there; they knew I would try to help them get over any problem by basically being a friend and just being there for them. I still hadn't had sex with anyone from school except for Kayla, and actually felt far better about whom I was and what I was doing here, rather than at any of my other hangouts.

This all began to change one afternoon when the newspaper editor, Michelle, told me she had an assignment for me. During the upcoming summer an extension would be added to the school, and the district decided to cut down the huge magnolia tree standing in the center of the student garden. The garden itself would also be removed in order to make way for a few more classrooms. Michelle asked me to take pictures of these soon-departed items for a front page story in the next issue. She begged me to make sure the finished results told an amazing story, like she knew I could do.

While I was taking these pictures, a strong crosswind began to blow through the courtyard and it actually made the tree branches look as though they truly understood what was to happen to them and were trying desperately to run away. These black and white photos were probably the best ones I ever shot.

An eerie feeling came over Michelle as she looked through my pictures. She assured me these were the pictures she wanted on the front cover and that I would get a fantastic byline, written just for me.

A week before an upcoming soccer game, Kayla put up a gigantic poster on my locker, just like she had many times before. This time the poster had soccer balls in the middle of a field of flowers, pink and white roses. It seemed odd to me at first, but that was Kayla. In the corner of the field there was a saying: *To those who tend, rewards will follow.* Again, I thought the saying was strange, but I knew Kayla always had a way with words. I interpreted the message to mean a goalie tends his little area of the field, and that we would win the game.

A third, seemingly unrelated incident happened the following day. We had potted flowers growing in the library that the librarian normally took care of. I was always staring at them while I studied as it helped me feel calm. She came over to me and said, "Phil, I'm going on vacation for a week and need someone to tend to the flowers. I hear you're real good with roses, so will you watch over them for me?"

None of these events appeared to be connected until that Friday. I was eating lunch with Billy when two senior girls approached our table. One of them looked at me quizzically and asked, "Are you the gardener?"

Both Billy and I laughed since neither of us had absolutely any idea what they were talking about. That's when they shared this amazing story with us and it all became perfectly clear, at least to me.

One of them said, "There's a sign in the senior girls' locker room. It says there's a guy who can make anyone's first sexual experience the best ever. The poster doesn't list a name, but says to look for a sign or symbol coming soon which will be revealed to those girls who are truly interested. The last line says to look for the gardener, and to make sure to get the school paper this Friday."

They handed me the edition of *The Weekly Beat* and it became very apparent as to why they thought I was the gardener.

The initial clue was located on the front page. My pictures of the magnolia tree and the garden were there. Underneath them was the byline the editor gave me. It read: *Carefully taken pictures reveal our sensitive subjects. Pictures supplied by the secret gardener.*

The second clue was in the sports section. There was a full page story about me explaining how I had won the last soccer game single-handedly and underneath the story was a close-up picture of the poster Kayla put on my locker. Everyone could read the saying: *To those who tend, rewards will follow.*

The final clue showed a picture of me and the flowers in the library with a caption that read: *Caring hands help cultivate new beginnings.*

Any interested girl could have easily put those three things together and figured out the answer.

I was blown away, I only knew of one person who could have arranged this. I found Kayla later that day and asked her about the whole thing. She said, "Sex is a big discussion in the girls' locker room. When there's someone like you who can make someone else feel so comfortable about their first time that information has to be shared. I just couldn't keep the secret any longer."

She smiled at me and added, "You know you're careful, and ya know how to keep feelings out of the mix. Besides, you told me you were comin' to grips with this side of you. I just wanted you to help some of my new friends feel the same way you made me feel. That gift you have must be shared."

Selfishly I admit, I understood her and readily agreed to help out her friends. She was to set up dates during the week and I would show up to do what she called "my magic."

Over the next few weeks, Kayla set me up with some virgin friends of hers from our school. I treated them with all the respect and caring I could muster. Kayla thought she was helping her friends and I believed I helped these girls in some way or another. But afterward I wasn't feeling so good about what I had done, so I let them all know I would never say anything to anyone—*I was now hiding another set of secrets.* But recalling girls love to talk about their experiences, I had no idea where this would lead.

I just wanted others to feel as special as Phil made me feel. I knew he was a sensitive and respectful first lover. I knew that no one would get hurt or pregnant by him—he would never allow that to happen because he cares way too much. And even if something did go wrong, somehow he would make it all work out just fine.

I was sure Phil liked what he was doing because it was helping the girls ... that's what he truly was all about.

Almost all of my friends thanked me for being introduced to Phil, although a few didn't. Take Peggy for instance.

I'm a friend of Kayla. I met her shortly after she dated Phil and went to the rink with him. She explained her experience with Phil and I wanted the same thing. I was very nervous when Phil showed up. There were all these scary thoughts running through my head, as I had only heard about what could happen the first time. I should have known Phil had it all planned out. We went to a drive-in—not really where I had planned on losing my virginity—but he made it special all the same. He was informative, he was gentle, and he instantly made me feel relaxed. There was no pain since he was so slow and considerate. He even had brought along some small moist towels to help me 'feel clean' after it was over.

I know some of the girls became more sexually active after being with Phil and developed an easy-going attitude about it, but I never did. I enjoyed our time together, but I realized sex was better left for those who are engaged or married, and certainly much more mature than high school students. No regrets, just discovery.

Chapter 26 — Monica

It didn't take long for me to find out this secret was already out and about—and even beyond the boundaries of school. One night after a soccer game I was approached from behind by an older female who I didn't know. She whispered in my ear, "I know who you are, and what you're doing."

I was petrified; I thought I was in big trouble, and in some ways I was.

She continued, "You're the guy my younger sister has been chattin' on the phone about. You're the hot topic of all her girly gossip and I'm curious to know why."

I was scared, but at the same time pleased her sister was saying good things about me.

"Let's see how you handle yourself around a real lady."

Well, she certainly didn't beat around the bush.

"Uh … I need to think this over," I said. "Let me get back to you later this week."

She handed me what looked like a business card, except it only had her name and phone number printed on it. She turned and started walking away, but called over her shoulder, "Kayla knows all about me … talk to her."

So I called Kayla that night and explained my reservations.

"Phil, don't blow this chance," Kayla insisted. "Monica knows her way around a bedroom. You'll get to be the student for once, instead of always being the mentor."

***

I met Monica at a quaint little Italian restaurant that was near where she lived. We sat down across from each other and she ordered a glass of red wine. I asked for a glass of lemonade.

"I'm twenty-one years old and just dropped out of St. Louis University," Monica stated. "I don't have many friends in the area, so when I heard about you as I was eavesdropping on my kid sister I wanted to see for myself."

She continued talking, but never asked any personal questions about me.

When we finished eating, she had me follow her to her apartment. After we walked in, she put some slow music on. Monica reached for one of my hands and silently led me to her bedroom. Without as much as one word, she undressed both of us. I could tell she was very comfortable with what was about to happen—this time it was *me* who wasn't as sure.

After a short session of preliminary kissing, she sank on the bed, pulling me down on top of her. I began exploring every part of her body and we moved in total unison. About an hour later, when I thought we were finished, she surprised me with a question, "Do you know what the G-spot is?"

When I said I had no idea what she was talking about, she took my hand and helped me discover another new erogenous zone for women. It took a couple of tries to locate this special place as she explained it all to me. After I found the magic spot and started to gently massage it with my finger, she let me know I was doing it correctly by having a volcanic orgasm.

As we lay next to each other, Monica lit up a cigarette. Exhaling a plume of smoke, she said, "I really appreciate it when a guy understands that the woman's pleasure needs to come first, before his own. We also like to have doors opened for us, and the chair pulled out at dinner. Not because we're helpless and can't do it on our own— it's not an ego thing either. It's just the actions that assure us we're in the company of a gentleman."

I guess I was a gentleman after all as I always did what she just explained.

While I drove home that night replaying all the scenes in my head, I came to realize no matter how much I thought I knew about the female sex, if I was open to letting new people into my life, there will always be someone who can teach me something new.

***

My confidence at school changed after Kayla's "intervention." Because she let my secret out, I was able to use it more as the girls started talking to their friends. Instead of just being there for these girls while at school, I began using the two drive-ins to listen to a whole new set of girls and to have sex with those who asked me for it.

Even though I enjoyed being with, and helping them find themselves, at the same time I was beginning to tire of it. It had been another long stretch of time since I felt the warm surge run through my heart, and I wondered why.

I began to feel the time had come for me to find my "one and only" girl and to experience true love. I had no idea where I would meet this girl as the ones I knew, or those who knew of me, already had those preconceived expectations of me. So I began to spend more time alone in my room again, just like when I started out on this journey years earlier. The hours I spent there this time was to think about what I had become, why I did what I did, and whether it was morally right or wrong. I prayed for some guidance.

Chapter 27 — Sally

It was the end of a long quiet night and I was totally lost in thought as I skated alone around the almost deserted rink. A girl skated up to me and said hi, so I instinctively said hi back without even looking up. She slid her arm around my waist and laughingly asked, "Are you that good-looking guy they call Disco Phil?"

I was still in my trance, but realized I recognized her unique laugh. I turned my head and was pleased to see it was my old friend from bowling.

I gave her a big hug and said, "Sally, what are you doing here? I never expected to see you anywhere except at bowling every week."

"Well, one of my friends was here last week and told me about this guy who wore fancy disco clothes and had the whole place eating out of his hand. I wanted to come see for myself and what a surprise when I saw it was you."

We laughed and started to share a couple's skate together. I always skated backwards to a couple's skate so I could see directly into the girl's eyes. I had looked into Sally's eyes in the past, but this time as I gazed into them I witnessed something I'd never seen before, not only did she have the beautiful sparkle of trust in them, she also had the sex gleam radiating at me.

Sally leaned in closer to me and whispered, "Last week you took my friend to a parking lot and she said it was fantastic sex. I'm very surprised, you only knew her for a night, but you've known me for eleven years and …"

While she didn't finish the sentence, I knew what she was hinting at. I'd never thought of Sally in this way and didn't know she thought of me like that either.

She broke the tension with a smile. "Now I've already thought all of this through. I trust and respect you, I know you won't hurt me, and I think this may even strengthen our friendship, so I need two things from you—I want you to be my first and I want it to happen tonight."

The feeling in my gut told me not to go through with it. Still, I agreed to what Sally wanted. *I had just let another girl make an important decision for me.*

When we got to the parking lot I reluctantly started my usual foreplay routine, although I wasn't thinking at all about Sally. I was wondering more about how this particular endeavor was going to affect me.

Normally I was able to empty my mind by going to my happy place so I could concentrate on how the girl was feeling. However, this time, I found myself contemplating the consequences that may arise from this. Because of this preoccupation, I didn't give it my all, but Sally didn't seem to notice. The entire time we were doing it she had a great big smile on her face, and seemed to be enjoying her first time.

After we finished, I noticed a difference in her. It started out when I saw her smile quickly disappear and realized she was in deep thought.

"Is there something wrong?" I asked. "If I did everything right, you should be feelin' pretty good right about now."

"My body feels fantastic. I never knew that this would be how I felt," she replied. "But my mind is sorta messed up. I know I told you I could handle this, but now it seems like I can't. I have no remorse, but I'm wonderin' if this was a mistake after all."

I *knew* this was going to happen. My gut was right again, but I didn't listen to it. I had missed a gigantic sign. I apologized to Sally, not for what we just shared, but more for feeling like I had taken advantage of a real friend.

I had always liked Phil. He was fun and easy to talk to. Even at bowling the little courteous things he did made me feel special. I had fantasized about him and making love, but never imagined that it would actually happen. When I asked him about it on the skating floor he seemed reluctant, like he knew it was a bad idea. But as I continued to press him, he finally gave in.

The feeling he gave me was fantastic. The physical sex was great, at least for me, but what did I have to compare it to? What it did to my head wasn't worth the trouble though. Phil quickly sensed that something was wrong and as we discussed it he apologized, even though it was me who forced it on him.

We continued to be friends afterward, but I felt a little part of us—the innocence, the camaraderie we had shared together as kids—had vanished because of this "adult thing" we did. I learned the hard way that sometimes it's better just to be friends with someone, and to keep fantasies safely stored away in the section of my brain where no one can ever get hurt.

***

After Sally, I was torn; I was making most of the girls happy with what we did, but felt as though I was hurting myself in the process. I realized I didn't feel good about my life any more. I also realized, once again, the girls were actually the ones in control and I was just giving them whatever they wanted, regardless of my true feelings.

For the first time, I seriously began to think what I was doing was indeed wrong; and I asked God for some help or forgiveness, though I never received a response.

Deep inside I knew what I needed. I wanted the commitment of a single relationship, one that could continue to grow stronger with time. I desperately wanted only one girl, the one I could finally give a red rose to, and for once have her understand the true meaning behind it.

I decided it was time to change what I was doing. Using the lessons the way I had been needed to come to an end.

And as these purer thoughts raced through my mind, I noticed two things happening. One was the warm feeling flowing through my heart, and secondly, outside the rain started coming down in buckets ... maybe God was listening to me after all.

I decided to go out and dance in the rain just like Nana and I had in the long-ago past. And as I was twirling around in circles, I swear the scent of mint made its way into my wet nostrils.

Chapter 28 — Kim

I made a firm commitment to take some time off from my current life and all the girls in it. I needed some alone time to just think, without all the commotion. I still wanted to skate as it did help me relax, so I decided to try a new rink, The Arch, where I knew no one and, more importantly, no one knew me. I still dressed the part of Disco Phil and still felt a confident presence, but I wasn't going to exploit it.

I was skating alone in my own little dream world when a girl rolled up to me, waved and said hi. I really wanted to be alone, but returned the same gesture. When I actually took the time to look up, I saw the most beautiful girl I'd ever seen. She was as tall as I was, had long blonde hair, and the most stunning blue eyes. They reminded me of the color of the ocean. I didn't even notice, nor cared, if she had the gleam or not. She was wearing faded blue jeans and an old Bob Seeger and the Silver Bullet Band t-shirt. I was smitten right then and there.

Even though she looked so good, I came here to be left alone. So as she started to talk to me, all I heard was, "My name is Kim ... *blah-blah* ... I'm a cheerleader at *blah-blah* High School ... I always skate here on Sunday nights since I have no school commitments ... *blah-blah.*"

When she asked me in rapid succession, "Where'd you learn to skate so well ... Where do you go to school ... Why are ya alone?" I answered her without any feeling. When she popped off another question which I didn't hear and didn't answer, she skated off.

I watched her talk with her friends for a while and then the shortest of them, Tina, skated over to me and asked, "Why are you so stuck up? How could you blow off Kim like that? Every guy here wants her to talk to them and, for some reason, she picked you. You know all she wants to do is skate with ya, not get married or anything."

That was basically the same thing Lisa told me about Mary, and I knew how that ended. I skated back up to Kim and said, "I'm sorry if you feel like I blew you off. I have way too many things on my mind tonight. I really just wanted to be alone, but I would like to get to know you. Why don't you tell me about yourself?"

She smiled and said, "I can relate to that. But before I leave you to yourself, I want you to know that I like disco music, too, and I really like the way you're dressed. Is there any chance I could get your phone number, so we can talk later?"

We exchanged numbers, and then I decided it was time for me to leave.

While I changed out of my skates and into my street shoes, I began to ponder. I had come here to be alone, yet, again, I met someone. It seemed as though I couldn't be by myself out in the world even if I wanted to be. Even without having a girl around me, I still attracted new ones. I wondered what I possessed that made them attracted to me. I decided they all thought I was confident and in control of my life, while the real truth of the matter was I was confused and beginning to experience a lot of self-doubt again. As I headed for my car, I seriously had no idea if I was going to call Kim or not.

I was skating with my friends when I saw him for the first time. He was cute and was dressed differently than anyone else in the rink. He had a confident air about him. When I started to talk to him he ignored me, which turned me on even more. Most boys fell over themselves if I even batted an eye at them.

A little later he came back and we started connecting. We had many things in common so it was easy to talk to him, when he wanted to listen. Again, I didn't understand why he was so distant, but it was working for me.

At the end of the night, I gave him my number and he gave me his. I thought it may end there but I wanted to know more about this mysterious guy so I knew I had to take matters into my own hands.

***

Kim was the one who made the first move; she called me the following night. Talk about not wasting any time! Even though she initiated the call, I started the conversation by immediately asking, "Why'd ya skate up to me in the first place?"

"I thought you were cute," she responded without hesitation. "You were quiet, but you looked friendly enough, and you had this air around you that said you were in control. There was just something that drew me to you."

We continued talking when I began to feel something I never had before. I felt as though I had developed the sparkle of trust in *my* eyes.

I needed to let this girl to know all about the good and the bad sides of me, and see what her response would be. "I was at your rink alone to veg out. I have some decisions to make and the music helps me think better. That's why, when you started to talk to me, I wasn't listenin' very well … I was lost in my thoughts. Right now, I feel lonely and very confused about my life. It all started a long time ago when my parents got divorced. It changed my personality at that time, and now that I finally seem to be back to *normal*, I haven't a clue if what I'm doing is right or wrong. At the rink where I usually skate I'm very popular, and I find myself doing things that girls want me to do in order to stay that way. I just wanted to get away and try to find myself again."

Kim had listened intently, and then said softly, "I totally understand.

Misguided Sensitivity

I sometimes feel the same way."

We made mostly small talk and then agreed to meet at The Arch again on Sunday. That night, as we skated together, it felt as though we were the only two people in the world that mattered. I did get to meet some of her friends, but forgot their names right after we were introduced. When I left for the night, I gave Kim a big thank-you hug and told her I'd call later in the week.

Driving home that night, I made up my mind I wanted Kim to be that steady girlfriend I was looking for. I was ready to give up everything I was doing just to be with her, and only her. She gave me a different type of confidence, one that resembled how I felt back when Mary and I were dating. I was proud of this feeling and I prayed to God Kim would see things the same way.

***

Later that week I called Kim. When she answered the phone she was crying. I got her to calm down and she explained, "I just learned that my parents are getting a divorce. I'm lost and don't know what to think. I feel terribly lonely right now. I know I'm askin' a lot, but can you come over so we can talk face to face?"

I arrived twenty minutes later. We sat on the balcony overlooking her small town and I let Kim do all the talking. When she finally cried her last tear, she looked at me and with a distinct sparkle in her eyes said, "I feel as though I can tell you anything. I don't know why I trust you so much. I feel like you're my closest friend right now and that's strange since you're also my newest. I don't understand these feelings I'm having for you and I'm scared it might be love. Can we go out, not to the rink, but somewhere else? Where do like to take a girl on a date?"

I nodded we could go, but I was a little scared myself that it could be love, so I said, "I normally go to the drive-in movies, but I don't think we should start there."

Kim looked at me strangely. "Why not? I'm game."

She waited for an answer. I decided to be honest and blunt. "I normally go there to have sex with a girl. I'd really like to get to know you first, so I'd prefer to go somewhere else."

Kim smiled back, unfazed by my candor, "Just because you did what ya did in the past doesn't mean you have to do it in the future. Like I said before, let's go to the drive-in, I'm game."

This whole conversation came as a surprise to me. Here was the girl I felt I wanted to be with, not knowing her inner feelings, but she just told me she'd be fine going to the drive-in with me, even knowing what may happen. As I pondered this thought, I wondered if this was really Kim or just the loneliness she was feeling inside doing the talking. Either way, I felt I was getting closer to what I wanted.

***

Kim and I went to the Twilight that week, as it was closer to her house than the Dirty Thirties, not to mention it didn't have the same "baggage" attached to it. We sat on opposite sides of the bench seat and watched the whole first movie in total silence. There was an awful tension in the car and both of us felt it. During the intermission I said in frustration, "What's wrong? You said you wanted to come here, and now you won't even sit next to me. I'm very confused. Whaddaya want from me?"

Kim stared back at me with her puppy dog eyes, "I was hopin' you'd make the first move. I've never been to a place like this with a boy, and I don't know what to do. I do know I wanna make out with you though, can you do somethin' to help me feel more comfortable?"

I relaxed a little, reached for Kim's hand and asked her to slide next to me, then I slowly started to kiss her. Within seconds the tension lifted. I was beginning to feel like she wanted more, so I started roaming her body with my hands, then slowly French kissing her. She was a little apprehensive, but as I continued to put all my feelings into it, eventually Kim began to respond favorably.

I continued to explore further when Kim nervously whispered into my ear, "I'm a little scared as to where this is gonna end up. I wanna experience it, but please be slow and listen to me. When I say stop, please stop. I'll trust you, but you need to respect me."

"You can trust me, this is all for you," I promised. "We will go at your pace, and you are in total control. Let me know what you want me to do and I'll respect what you say."

Kim relaxed when I said that and let me start touching her breasts through her shirt. She was breathing hard but seemed fine with it, so I took another step. I slowly undid the buttons on her shirt and took it off. Even slower, I undid her bra, put it on the seat next to us, and started to caress and kiss her breasts. I felt Kim nervously squirm in her seat, but she didn't stop me.

I had no idea where this was leading us either. This time I was thinking only about Kim and what her reactions would be. I wanted to show her everything I knew, but felt she may not be ready for it all at once. As I continued to escalate my moves, I found myself talking to Kim, explaining what I was going to do next, and asking her permission before I went through with it. I wanted this to be special for her. I also realized I wanted it to be special for me, too.

I had no idea what to expect when we got to the movies. I thought I was ready, but my actions proved me wrong. After talking it through, Phil was so slow and understanding. Everything he did was new to me. I liked the feeling, but was scared. When he first touched my breast I jumped a little. He calmed me down by talking me through what he was doing and actually asked if I was okay with it first. Since I never had experienced this before I had no idea where this was leading, but I couldn't wait to find out.

Since Kim hadn't told me to stop I continued to raise the stakes. I moved one of my hands to her thigh, and then between her legs. As I started to rub her vagina through her pants, I felt the heat of passion come straight through to the surface. Kim moved against my rubbing movements, resulting in even more friction. When I slowly undid her belt, I felt Kim's breath become more defined. I undid the top button of her jeans and then unzipped them. I slowly slid my hand into her jeans to rub her panties and Kim moved her head closer to my neck. I felt her hot breath as she breathed on my neck. I moved my hand closer to get inside her panties and I quietly asked, "Do you want me to stop?"

Her answer was to spread her legs wider, as if inviting me inside. After I found her "special spot" she began to kiss my neck harder and harder. Not long after I began touching her, a tremor went through her body. "What was that feeling? I've never felt quite like that before."

I smiled at her and said, "Welcome to the world of internal orgasms."

Kim asked me what was next. Much to my own surprise, I said that was all for now. I helped her get dressed, and then we cuddled through the rest of the second movie.

I was trembling with excitement. I was both scared and excited. Phil helped me through the mixed feelings I was having by being sensitive and gentle. When he touched me I felt my body heat rise. I had never felt like that before. When I climaxed that way for the first time, he knew what it was, and was excited that he helped me reach it. I thought for sure I was going to lose my virginity that night, but he stopped. He let me experience things at my own pace. I began to gain more respect for him because of his understanding. What other guy would put my feelings over his own? I wanted him, but didn't know how to tell him.

After dropping off Kim, I drove home thinking about what just happened. As a rule I would have had sex with the girl and then forget about her. This time around what I experienced with Kim got me even more excited than if I actually would have had sex with her. It was then I realized I didn't want to have sex with Kim; I wanted to *make love* to her, and I wanted to make a real connection.

***

Kim and I went back to the Twilight again the following week. This time, though, she was different. After she entered my car, she quickly slid next to me, gave me a big wet kiss, and wanted to start making out immediately. While we drove, I said, "I feel you're different tonight, but before we start anything I need to talk to you."

I *wanted* to explain to Kim how I felt. I *wanted* her to know I thought I loved her, and hoped for a one-on-one relationship with her. I *wanted* her to know I didn't just want sex from her. I *wanted* her to know I didn't want to mess this up. I *wanted* to do all of this, but couldn't bring myself to say any of it.

I looked at her and could only muster, "Are you sure you're ready for this?"

She smiled back and excitedly replied, "Not only am I ready, but I'm willing and able, too."

After getting settled at the drive-in, when I started my routine, this time it was different for me. I was more into it than ever before. I really felt what I was doing, not just going through the motions. It was even better than my time with Stacey.

Just as I wanted Kim to feel good physically, I wanted myself to feel better mentally. I was sure Kim had no idea what was going on in my head. I was able to feel every movement we made, every breath we shared, and every shiver both Kim and I experienced. I knew by these feelings, that for the first time in my life, I was *finally making love*. When it came to an amazing end, I found myself crying.

Kim asked me why and I explained, "Tonight I've found someone I can share the pleasure of making love with. This wasn't just sex to me, I feel like I'm truly wanted, not just needed. I'm extremely happy right now."

I opened my glove compartment and handed Kim a red silk rose; this time the rose stood for love. I'm sure Kim didn't totally understand, but I knew I felt very good about myself for the first time in a very long time.

Because making love felt so much better than just having sex, I finally felt as though I actually mattered to someone. I believed Kim and I were perfect for each other and started to believe I had finally found the few things I always wanted from a female; a steady girlfriend, a long-term relationship, and an understanding of what true love should be. I loved Kim with my whole body, my whole mind, and ultimately with my whole heart. Those shaky walls around my heart came shattering down.

This was the moment I dreamed about. I laid back and let Phil take my virginity. He knew so much more than I did. I enjoyed myself and it was wonderful. I hoped he felt the same way. For some reason, when it was over, he was the one crying. As he explained why, I didn't totally understand any of it. It took me by surprise as I had never seen a boy cry before. I wondered where this was leading us next. I couldn't explain it at the time, but I immediately knew that we had totally different ideas about that.

Kim and I dated for a few more months. We shared many more nights of pleasure together. I thought I loved her and it appeared she loved me back. Unfortunately, what I learned instead was Kim had used me just like so many of the other girls before her. She only needed someone to be there for her while she was going through some difficult times and once again, I was the chosen one.

When she officially broke up with me, Kim said, "I hope I haven't hurt you too much. You were there for me when I needed you to be and I thank you for that. You showed me things, and made me feel things that I never had before, you were very good for me. I just don't think we're right for each other because we want two completely different things out of life. You wanna settle down, and I wanna explore. I feel like you let your emotions rule your life too much, a real man would never cry over what he felt. I need a stronger man who can take care of me and my needs, now that you've opened them up to me."

I didn't want to hurt Phil, but it was crystal clear to me that we didn't want the same things. The timing was off. He was ready to end his journey and mine was just starting. Now that he helped me experience sex and I knew, with the right attitude, it wouldn't hurt me; I wanted more of the same from a variety of other men

Phil had told me about his unending line of young girls who he thought had just used him. What he never understood was that these girls were just smart enough to know that they were too young to fall for the first guy who made them feel good about themselves. I was the same. I wanted to make sure I, too, had a buffet of sexual experiences so I would know for sure when I had found my "one and only" true love.

While he was sweet and sensitive to my needs, I saw something else. Phil was a man, he was looking for a "shirt" that he could wear every day for the rest of his life, but he was dealing with girls, young girls at that, and you know how we love to shop and compare ... one dress will never do.

I wanted to explain all this to Phil, but something inside told me it'd be better if he discovered it—soon I hope, for his sake—on his own.

***

I should've known better. I went against one of the things I promised myself not to do: I let someone get into my heart. I felt a pain I hadn't since Mary moved away. I stupidly gave Kim not only my body and my soul, but also my heart, and now I was dearly paying the price. The walls around it, which had come down so fast, were quickly built up again, only this time higher and stronger, and I promised myself I would never let them come down again.

Unfortunately I now felt the best way to forget Kim was to go back to my mechanical one-night stands. At least I could help other girls have some enjoyment in their lives, even though I wasn't enjoying mine.

Chapter 29 — Betty

After Kim left me it was as though I was living in a sort of unfeeling fog. I was able to go back to The Roller Wheel to skate, but I sure had a different aura around me. The confident air I once possessed was replaced by a large dark cloud of self-doubt. I was confused and lonelier than ever. One of the girls who noticed this was Betty.

Betty and I were casual friends; we skated together, we talked together, and sometimes we laughed together. One thing we weren't was interested in each other sexually. Betty wasn't your typical teenage girl; she was plain to look at, with long stringy brown hair which she never seemed to wash, she was a little overweight and wore raggedy old clothes. Essentially, she didn't really care about her appearance, nor what people thought about her. Looking into her eyes you could see they were gray and dull. They told me she never, ever thought about sex. She basically kept to herself and was just fine with that. She knew all about my escapades at the rink, but never judged me. She did say one day I would meet my match and that it just may kill me.

On one of these difficult nights when I was too busy thinking about my life to notice anything else, Betty skated up to me and asked, "Hey what's up? You've lost a step or two. I really liked watching the old, arrogant you when ya thought you were in total control of everything. It was fun to see what kind of trouble you'd get into. What happened, did someone new steal your heart?"

"Yeah, she did. You told me if I played with fire that one day I'd get burned, well welcome to that day," I said sadly. "I actually thought it was love, but I just got played again."

Betty became sympathetic. "I was just kidding. I'm sorry about what happened. Getting hurt is a part of life, but that's why the girls here like you so much, *you never hurt anyone*. They get what they need from you and don't have to think about anything else. Most guys would kill to be in your position, so why should a girl think you've got any problem with it?"

She paused as if she was debating something, then said, "I can't believe I'm saying this, but ... I think you should go back to those one-nighters, it gives you confidence and makes you who are you are. You're not the same person without them."

I gave Betty a big hug as I concurred she was right. I was going back to my old self, whether it was right or wrong, only this time *my* needs were going to be a priority, too. I thanked Betty by gently kissing her on both cheeks and proudly said, "Promise me that you'll call when you're ready to lose your virginity!"

She laughed and said, "Welcome back, stud!"

Phil and I had been friends at the rink. He was nice, honest, and trusting. But he was also so naive. He would do anything for anyone, and never thought about taking care of his own feelings. I didn't agree with what Phil was doing, but when I saw how he'd lost his confidence, I wanted to help. After our talk it was neat to see his confidence coming back. But to be honest, I really don't know if I gave him the right advice.

Chapter 30 — Beverly

After my talk with Betty I did go back to my old ways and, in fact, I was able to go back to The Arch, the very same rink where I met Kim, just to prove to myself I was over her. That's where I met Beverly.

Beverly had been there every Sunday back when I skated with Kim. I noticed she always skated with a small circle of friends and rarely ever talked to anyone else. Now, normally girls approached me, but this time I decided to take the initiative. I looked her over and noticed she was tall and lanky, somewhat plain-looking, but with a glow that made me want to meet her. She was older than many of the girls I knew, but thanks to my recent experience with Monica, this didn't intimidate me as much it probably should have.

This particular night she was alone when I skated up to her and nonchalantly asked, "Would you like to skate with me?"

She looked apprehensive, but replied, "Sure, but first let's talk."

We sat on the bench overlooking the rink and she told me, "My name is Beverly and I'm twenty-four years old. I know who you are because the girls here all talk about you. It seems like they missed you when you left. But what I want to know is, what happened to that cute blonde you used to skate with?"

I was surprised she knew of me and my ex-girlfriend. "Let's just say she got what she wanted and leave it at that. It was a painful experience for me, I thought I was in love, but I just got hurt again. I'm over her now, so let's talk about you."

Beverly nodded her head as if she knew this feeling herself. "I understand the hurt, I've been there before, that's why I do things differently than other girls do."

She didn't elaborate on what she meant, and I didn't press the issue. We agreed to meet every Sunday night for skating only. There would be no dates at the drive-ins, and Beverly never showed any interest in me, except to skate with. I tried using some of my lessons with Beverly, but many of them didn't work. She didn't talk all that much, so I couldn't listen and remember the little things about her. I didn't try to use my emotions at all to connect with her. It didn't appear she had any clear cut wants or needs. And I never saw the trust sparkle, or the sex gleam, come to her eyes.

She was an excellent skater, though, so I presumed she just enjoyed having a good skate partner, and that was it. Thus, I was somewhat surprised when she asked me to her house one Sunday night after skating.

After following her into the living room, she nervously asked,

"Would you like something to drink?"

"Do you have any white wine?" I quickly inquired.

"That surprises me," she smiled. "I thought you'd be more of a beer man. But luckily, all I drink is white wine."

After downing a few cold glasses, Beverly brought out a joint and lit it. She motioned for me to take a puff, and I did. I never smoked pot before, but had seen others enjoy it at the parking lot, and I really liked the smell. She turned on her stereo and I was surprised to hear jazz flow from the speakers, just like I'd heard when I was with Deidre. Maybe it had something to do with them being older.

The pot went straight to my head and I started to lose control of my senses. For a while I didn't know where I was, what I was doing, or why. Even though others seemed to like these effects, I knew right away I would never smoke again. I needed to be in control of myself at all times.

I opted to stop smoking, but Beverly had one more joint. After putting the last bud out, Beverly unexpectedly kissed me, long and passionately. I went along with it; between the wine, the joint, and the music, I was feeling no pain.

I took this as a sign to initiate sex even though Beverly told me before she didn't do what the other girls did. But as I slowly began to unzip her pants, she stopped me. "I'm so sorry I've led you on. You need to know I was recently hurt very badly. Until I'm over him, I won't allow myself to have sex. I know you're feeling the urge, but I really can't do this right now."

I was confused. "So why'd you invite me over, offer me wine and pot, and put on romantic music? Obviously, you led me to believe sex is what you wanted from this."

Beverly looked at me with a twinge of guilt. "I watched you with that blonde on many a Sunday night and wondered what you did with her to make her smile so much. I want to experience that feeling again myself someday, but it can't be tonight. Let me help you instead."

Beverly undid my pants and proceeded to go down on me. I had never been in this position before; I was always the one giving the pleasure, not directly receiving it. While Beverly continued, I felt as though she had done this many times before and thoroughly enjoyed doing it, so I just closed my eyes, listened to the music, and let the alcohol and pot take its full effect on me.

When it was over, Beverly eagerly smiled at me and asked, "How was that?"

I was a little dazed by it all and mumbled, "Thanks pretty lady for making me feel like I normally make the girl feel."

Beverly seemed content we didn't have sex and although I was happy to experience something new, at the same time I began to feel awkward about the role reversal. Wasn't I the one who was always supposed to make the girl feel good?

After a debate with myself, I was able to add to my list:

16) It is better to give ... but be willing to receive when it's your turn.

Chapter 31 — Tina

One Thursday night a few weeks later at the Arch, I had tired of skating and was sitting on a bench listening to the grainy, organ music which they always played. It had a unique sound that echoed through the high rafters of the old building. It reminded me of sitting long ago in the archaic church I detested so much, where I first heard the weekly lessons of "right and wrong."

My mind wandered back to Nana and how she, too, didn't believe in the importance of any designated place to worship. The wonderful visions I used to get of my dear Nana had stopped appearing to me, and I wondered why. I found myself thinking, *I really could use some of her grandmotherly advice in my life right now.*

I was jarred back to reality when a girl flashed by me and shouted, "Hi" over the music. She was gone before I could even blink, but as I watched her circle the rink, I found myself absolutely mesmerized by her. She was cute, extremely short, and had long black hair she had tied up with a yellow bow. She was wearing a yellow tank top which was covered by a lighter yellow blouse, and the short shorts she was wearing were very tight and also very yellow. I laughed out loud as I found myself thinking she was a human symbol for friendship, and I decided to take her up on her not so subtle message.

My eyes followed her around the rink a few times more before I decided I had been idle too long. I hopped onto the floor, caught up to her, and flashed my best smile. "Is it okay if I skate with you?"

She smiled back. "Of course you can, Phil. I'd never say no to you."

I thought I'd never met this girl, but she spoke to me as if we were old friends.

She saw the bewilderment on my face. "I'm a friend of Kim, and met you the very first night you skated here."

Even that explanation didn't jar my memory.

She continued in a confident tone, "I know everything you guys did and how badly she mistreated you afterward. I don't think she was very nice about it, but I do know she's now missin' the kind of excitement that so far she's only had with you."

I was happy to hear that and hoped maybe Kim might come back to me.

But the without missing a beat, and with the sex gleam pulsating from her eyes, she added, "Ya know it's gettin' very hot in here all of a sudden, so how about the two of us goin' to the Twilight?'

I saw him the minute he walked in. I was waiting for this night. I knew what

Misguided Sensitivity

my plan of action was. I said hi to him, but let him come to me. When he took the bait I knew what would happen next—thank you Kim—when I asked him to take me to the drive-in.

Clearly, Kim had told her everything, and now she wanted her turn. I pulled into the drive-in, and as soon as I put the car in *Park,* she took control. She had so monopolized the conversation I still hadn't had the time to ask her name. After we started doing it, she said, "You know, Kim told me how good you were and how much she enjoyed it, how you gave directions and she just followed along. Well, this time I'm gonna give *you* some directions and I want you to follow 'em, cuz I like things other girls don't."

I was completely overwhelmed by her aggressiveness as I resisted the urge to salute her.

Without any hesitation she said, "I want you to suck my fingers, nice and slow. And when you're done with that I'll show you how I like to make love ... not the typical man-on-top style I'm sure you're used to."

After I did everything she asked, including positions that made me feel like a human pretzel, and doing things I never thought I could in the back seat of a car, she said, "Wow, you take directions really well, that'll come in handy later."

"Of course I do," I replied, feeling a little embarrassed. "I've been listenin' to what girls want for my whole life." Then I thought to myself, *I wonder what I really want.*

When the sex was over, all she wanted to do was talk, talk, talk, on and on she rambled, "... and I come from a broken home ... I live with my grandmother .... I don't know either of my parents .... Most of my friends are people I meet at the rink .... I really like skating .... I think it's one of my favorite things .... By the way, my name is Tina."

I was trying to get a word in edgewise when she confessed, "Phil, this was all a set-up. I've been waiting for you to come back to the rink so I could have sex with you. After Kim told me all about you, I needed to try ya myself. I had a great time tonight, and I have another friend you *really* need to meet; trust me on this."

After I gave her a white silk rose, because I knew she was *way too young* to understand true love, Tina handed me a small slip of paper on which she had written the name *Nancy,* along with an address. She made me promise I would go see her later that week.

He did exactly what I wanted and needed him to do. He was even better than what Kim had said. He was more than competent and took directions very well. He didn't know it, but I had a plan for him.

I've been through a lot in my life, although I'm only sixteen. But my troubles always seem to go away when I have an experienced man inside me. There's a lot to be said for Phil's type of experience, so I really hope he follows through on my request for him to seek out Nancy. I think it will be good for him, and I know it will be good for "them."

Chapter 32 — Nancy

A few weeks later I was driving down Main Street and noticed I was close to the address Tina had written on the paper. I found the location and stopped. It turned out to be a Chicken Unlimited restaurant. When I asked the high school guy behind the counter for Nancy, I was expecting another high school age girl to emerge. I was a little taken back as a mature woman came out.

"Uh … I'm Phil." I mumbled, "Tina sent me to meet you."

Nancy laughed and then directed me to go sit in the lobby. "I'll be out when I can."

What was this all about? Why would Tina want me to meet an older lady, she had to be at least *thirty*? Although she was good looking, she had more wrinkles around her eyes than I'd ever seen and she looked a little weathered—like she'd led a very hard life and took her solace in drinking. Where was this leading me to?

I didn't have time to think this through as Nancy appeared and sat right next to me. "Wow, Phil," she exclaimed, "you're a young one, but you do have the looks. Tina only sends me top quality, so I'm sure you'll fit the bill."

I was confused as hell and got even more messed up as Nancy bluntly added, "I'm thirty-five years old, divorced, and I want to know if you'll have sex with me tonight?"

When I didn't answer right away, she waved her finger at me, "You need to remember one thing in life young man, whenever a lady asks you to have sex with her, you don't say no."

"I have a saying for this occasion," I instinctively replied. "Yes pretty lady, I can help you feel good."

It was only then, as Nancy patted my knee and nodded her approval of my comment I realized I'd somehow agreed to her outrageous invitation.

I knew Phil was going to be a hit when I first saw him. He was tall, skinny, young, and had a great ass. My women were going to eat him up. I had to break him in first myself so I was glad when he accepted my invitation for that night. Tina had never let me down before, so I was hoping this wasn't going to be the first time. I had a feeling Phil was going to be one of my best.

Nancy gave me an address and told me to show up at 7:00 pm. sharp. I left, shaking my head, not knowing what to expect from later that evening. While I was dressing that night I thought to myself, *What type of situation had I gotten myself into this time?*

I put on a purple silk shirt, a pair of black Angel Flight pants, and wore my gray cowboy boots. Looking into the mirror as I sprayed on my Musk Oil, I again saw what I thought was a pretty good looking young man staring back. But as I looked deeper into his eyes, for the first time I saw actual fear.

***

I knew I was getting comfortable again with the sex part of my life. I knew I wasn't going to let anyone else into my heart, and I knew because of that fact nobody would get hurt anymore. But, what I didn't know was what would a thirty-something divorced lady want from me?

Had I finally lost what was left of my young mind?

Reminding myself age shouldn't matter, I took a deep breath and decided to let whatever happens happen. I was going to try to enjoy the moment. I hoped the same would be true for Nancy.

When I rang the doorbell and Nancy answered wearing a sweatshirt and sweatpants, I felt overdressed. She had a lit cigarette in one hand and half a glass of red wine in the other. She looked me up and down and said, "Right on time, that's a good sign. Come on in. Tina wasn't lying— you do have one hot body to look at. Would you like something to drink?"

"How about white wine?" I shyly asked.

Nancy looked impressed. "That's an answer I like."

While we sat next to each other on her couch nursing our wine, she seductively asked, "How often do you have sex; where do you have it, and what do you like the most about it?"

When I replied to the last part, "I like to make the girls feel good," Nancy smiled. "That's another answer I like. You're doing just fine."

I felt like I was on a job interview or something. (Little did I know?)

"That's enough talk," she abruptly said. "Now let's go have sex. Tina told me you are fantastic, so I'm not trying to add any pressure on you, but I'm expecting something special."

This was totally absurd to me. I had a thirty-five-year-old lady talking bluntly about sex and what she expected from me. I was a barely seventeen-year-old guy who was going to try to make this obviously experienced lady's bell ring. As I gulped down the rest of my wine I said to myself, "God help me!"

He was so hot when I first saw him dressed up. Not only did he look good, but he already liked wine. That would go far when he met the others. They liked the finer things in life and so far he fit the bill. The only thing I would need to change was his cologne.

Misguided Sensitivity

Nancy led me to her bedroom where she put on a cassette and had me listen to the words of a song before we started. The song was *Let's Get It On* by Marvin Gaye.

Nancy said, "I wanted you hear and remember those words so you knew exactly how some women feel as they're looking for sex. To most people sex is a good thing, and sex is a fun thing, but some women have trouble finding what they need, hopefully someone sends them some help. In life, you must always remember all people really want is to share some quality time together. Do you understand me?"

While I shook my head yes, what I really meant was no.

With that out of the way, Nancy said it was now time for us to have sex—this I completely understood.

I started my routine, which I was so familiar and comfortable with and forgot all the weird stuff from earlier. I used all the kissing, the touching, and the feelings I learned from the other ladies in my life in this sexual experience. When we both had finished, over two hours later, Nancy calmly said, "Tina was absolutely correct, you're one of the best, and you'll fit in perfectly."

I finally had enough and demanded to know, "Fit into what? All night long you've been telling me how I would 'do nicely', how you liked my answers, and that the others would adore me. What the hell are you talking about?"

Nancy laughed and put a reassuring hand on my cheek. "Phil, I have many friends who are divorced or separated. They're all looking for that special someone to help them. Many just need someone to talk to, while others want even more. These special women are looking for a talented young 'stud' to help them experience life again. And since you have the looks, the sensitivity, the maturity, and the moves to help them, you can make us some good money at the same time."

Even in my wildest imagination, the idea that my "talent" might have monetary value had never occurred to me.

I just laid there with my mouth partially open as she continued, "You already know about some of the finer things in life, such as good music, fine wine, and how to dress properly. You know how to treat a lady, and it's obvious you know how to give great sex. If you use these talents the right way, the sky is the limit. *And* if you can keep love out of the mix, that will help both of us. These ladies of mine are more than happy to pay for gentlemanly companionship and we are happy to accept their money, so it all works out very nicely for everyone. You have a special gift, and you should be rewarded for giving it."

My head was spinning, not only from what she just said, but also because I had just given my all to a thirty-five-year-old and she thoroughly enjoyed it. All I really heard her say anyway was I could get paid for having sex. This was an opportunity to share my gift with ladies who would truly appreciate it, not the innocent young girls who couldn't really understand it. That was exactly what I was looking for ... I thought.

Over another glass of wine I agreed to her proposal, so we got down to business.

"You'll need to be available mostly Friday through Sunday. With husbands no longer in the picture, these ladies tend to get lonely on the weekends. But there will be a few week nights, and some may be on short notice, so I need you to be flexible."

"I'll set up all your appointments and tell you where to meet; most will start at The Plantation, a bar and restaurant where I know the owner. You'll have no problem getting in and ordering alcohol for the ladies, though you should always order a non-alcoholic drink for yourself. In the privacy of the ladies' homes, your drink-of-choice is up to you."

Nancy started to explain the financial arrangement but I stopped her. "I trust you, just like you obviously trust me. What else do we need to do to get this thing started?"

Nancy put on a serious face. "We need to talk about 'protection' and safety."

I thought she meant something totally different than what she started to explain. Nancy insisted I always use a condom, due to the problematic after effects if someone should have an STD.

I had just learned another valuable lesson from a lady.

When she was finished explaining things, she said, "Tomorrow we'll go shopping. I like your taste already and so will the ladies, so I'll just get you some more of the same. I do want to change your cologne. I believe 'Red for Men' is a better and more mature smell for you. I like your tiger pendant, but some of the ladies may not, so we we'll get you a shiny gold charm that has your astrology sign written in Greek on it. Finally, we have got to change that God awful Playboy bunny in your ear to something else. Let's get you a solid gold letter H instead. It will stand for *the healer.*"

***

Nancy set up my first meeting for that Friday. The first time was harder than I originally thought it would be. Since these ladies were older, it was a struggle to find things in common with them to talk about.

But from the second lady I met, I learned almost everything I needed to know. She taught me all about movies (chick flicks), fine jewelry, and gourmet food — all while I made her feel wanted again just by listening to

Misguided Sensitivity

her. Thanks to Terri and her advice, I remembered everything this lady told me.

It felt good to learn new things again and it got much easier each time I met a new lady. During this time, I met many new and exciting females. In my past, most of the girls I had been with were white, high school girls who were both too innocent and much too young to know what they wanted. That drastically changed as I started meeting these older women between the ages of thirty and fifty. They came from all races, religions, and backgrounds.

To my surprise, most of them just needed to talk to a guy who was a good listener, and who cared about what they had to say. Some only wanted someone to sit next to them while they went to the movies. Many needed a chaperone to a fancy party or dinner, a few just wanted to be seen in the presence of a male again, and of course others wanted the *whole treatment*.

These ladies were neither innocent nor lacking in the knowledge of what they wanted from me. *Now I knew why taking directions were so important.* And by *really* listening to what the ladies were implying, I was able to give them just what they wanted.

Whatever the reason they needed me was, I treated these women with the respect and sensitivity they deserved and tried to make them feel desirable again. I really felt as though I made a difference to them all. I gave them all white silk roses afterward to show them I would keep our times together a secret for their safety. *Another meaning of the white rose comes to light.*

***

I thought I was living a dream while sharing my gift. At the same time, these ladies genuinely respected and liked me. All of them taught me new things about life in general. And what these ladies reinforced for me was that we are truly all the same inside. Although we may all have different thoughts, different beliefs, and we may be on our own journey through life, I confirmed, once again, all of us just want to be accepted and happy. These liaisons taught me that sometimes we all need someone who cares to help us through.

There were countless faces that came into my life during this time, many who I don't remember. However, there were two ladies in particular from this vast array of women who I *do* remember, *and* for two diametrically opposite reasons.

Chapter 33 — Roxy

Nancy asked me to do her a special favor one night. She had a friend who was newly divorced and needed someone to help her get back on her feet. She was described to me as in her late thirties, very attractive, and *extremely* nervous. She had been married for a little under twenty years and had never been with anyone except her ex-husband.

Nancy needed me to be especially sensitive with this one. "Meet her at The Plantation in the back bar at 7:00. She's tall, with graying short black hair, and will look very distinguished. She'll have a blue dress on and a yellow flower in her hair. Her name is Roxanne. I told her that you were young, tall, and sexy. She knows you'll be wearing a purple shirt, black pants, and smell like Red for Men. I told her your name was DJ. Have fun, but please treat her extra special for me."

Nancy never let me use my real name for safety reasons; even though she knew all of these ladies, she always said, "You can never be too careful..."

I walked into the back bar of The Plantation — my normal meeting place — where the bartenders knew me and never gave me a problem about being underage and I recognized Roxanne right away. She was sitting by herself, sipping a wine cooler, and it was apparent she was indeed extremely anxious. I watched her for a few minutes as she constantly ran her long fingers through her hair, looked at herself in a small, round mirror, and basically behaved in an uncomfortable manner.

She wasn't as nervous as I had just become, though. I had to step back into the front bar to decide if I could go through with this. I realized she needed my help, and that was the only reason why I was there. Come what may, I decided to go through with the night.

As *Secret Agent Man* by Johnny Rivers played softly in the background, I slowly walked into the back bar, came up from behind Roxy, and covered her eyes.

I asked, "Who do you think this is?"

"I-I'm hoping its DJ," she stammered.

"That's right," I said, "but I have another surprise for you. Are you ready?"

She nervously nodded her approval so I walked around her so she could see who I was, uncovered her eyes, and said, "Surprise!"

When her eyes met mine, she blushed, and quickly threw back her drink.

This person, who I knew as Donna, was a friend of my mom. I had known her for many years. I thought about how people said it was a small world and that we're all connected somehow; this was my living proof of that.

I sat down and ordered her another drink. Still startled she asked, "How'd you get into this? Does your mom know this is how you spend your nights?"

"Of course not," It was my turn to blush, "and can we try to keep it that way, please?"

Donna and I continued to talk and the more we did, the more relaxed she became. We even danced together. She was slowly sipping her third drink when Donna confessed, "I need someone to make me feel special again. I've been feeling really down on myself since Hank left me. I don't think I have anything left to give to anyone. I've never been with anyone except Hank, and I haven't been on a date for over twenty years. God knows, I'm lost and all alone here in the real world, and I don't know where to turn."

"Tonight, turn to me," I said with amazing confidence. "You have the whole world to offer someone new. You're smart, you're pretty, and you're successful."

Donna blushed when I said that, but it seemed to relax her even more.

"Believe me, I know firsthand how sometimes this journey of life takes us to places we don't want to be, for reasons we may never understand," I said resolutely. "You'll make it just fine without Hank; it just may take some time. Have faith in God, and tonight have faith in *me*."

When we got up to dance again, Donna looked deep into my eyes and I saw both the sparkle of trust *and* the sex gleam staring back at me. "Phil or DJ, whoever you are tonight, I'm ready for the next step in my life. Could you please help by having sex with me tonight?"

There was that question again.

I answered the way Nancy would have wanted me to, "Yes pretty lady, I will help you feel good."

***

We were leaving when a song by Dr. Hook came on and we stopped to listen to it. We looked at each other, held hands, and shared a laugh when we heard the words, *sharing the night together*.

I followed Donna to the hotel Nancy had set up, and we shared *part* of the night together. When I was getting up to leave, she was sound asleep and I saw a great big smile on her face. I hoped it was because of me, and not from all the alcohol she drank.

I wrote Donna a nice little note saying I cared, that she would be just fine and that I would never tell anyone about our time together. I hoped she would do the same.

    I was feeling real bad about myself after my divorce. I needed someone to help convince me I was still attractive. As Nancy described DJ to me I actually felt excited. Then, when he arrived and stood before me I was shocked to see it was Phil. My first thought was, "Roxy, grab your purse, get the hell out of there, and pretend that this never happened." I knew his mom, for Pete's sake.
    After a few drinks, some eye-opening conversation, and finally some soul-searching, I fully understood why he did what he did. He treated me with such respect that I started to feel good about myself. As I watched the other ladies in the bar look lovingly at him, although I was scared, he made me feel like a young girl again, so I decided to go through with the original plans.
    In bed he knew just what to do and where to do it. Hank never treated me so well. Phil was considerate, warm, and understanding of my needs and the situation I was in. As we continued to make love, I felt all my problems float away.
    I fell asleep happy, and when I woke up I had to say I was relieved he was gone. In his place was a note and two flowers. That was so sweet of him. I have never told anyone that a seventeen-year-old boy made such an impact in my life.
    Interestingly, I recall a conversation I had with his mom a few months after Phil and I had our rendezvous. She was concerned about Phil. He was pulling away from her. She believed it was because of her marrying Bob. Phil was never home at night and she thought he was out getting into trouble. I tried to ease her mind. I said that knowing Phil, he was probably keeping someone else from getting into trouble. I told her I hoped someday to meet a man who understood people as well as her teenage son seemed to.

Chapter 34 — Cheryl

The other lady I'll never forget is Cheryl. You already know Nancy never let me use my real name for safety reasons. She also didn't want me talking too much about myself. I was there to make the ladies feel better, not to go on and on about myself. Unfortunately, Cheryl learned too much. She was twenty-eight, a divorced mother of two children, who had settled down too soon, and hated the situation she was in.

At first I thought things went well; we met, we danced, and we had sex. It must have gone very well because Cheryl booked the next three weeks with me. But on that third night, Cheryl looked me in the eyes and said, "DJ, I think I'm falling in love with you."

I quickly put a hand to her lips. "That can't happen. You aren't in love with me; you're in love with what I represent to you — freedom. What we share is simply sex. If you can't understand that, I think we need to stop meeting."

Cheryl pushed my hand away and said, "There's no way you can tell me you're not in love with me, look at what we've done the last few weeks. That means love to me."

I knew Cheryl was going to be trouble; she couldn't tell the difference between love and casual sex. And I thought only the younger girls were confused.

I immediately left, but she followed me, and found out where I lived. She started to track me everywhere I went; to school, to work, and to skating. When she started showing up at The Roller Wheel on Fridays, I got scared. She would stand off to the side and stare; all I could think of was that she was going to give my secret away and I would get into trouble. I called Nancy, but to my chagrin she said she couldn't help. I finally had no choice but to call the police and get a restraining order against Cheryl.

***

Man, was I upset! I was just trying to make a lady feel good and look what happened. This got me to thinking again about what I was doing on this part of my journey. I really enjoyed helping these ladies and was even starting to get very comfortable doing it, but now realized these experiences weren't helping me enough to continue. Although, I did develop a refined sense of style, a love of fine wine, an appreciation for a good "chick flick", and a giant boost in my confidence, the trade-off just wasn't worth it anymore.

I had met many interesting women and was able to experience many new things, but now I knew for sure I was doing it for the wrong reasons, just like I had been warned against. I was beginning to feel as though I was letting myself and God down, not to mention I felt as though my very soul had become blackened by what I was doing.

I felt much older than I actually was, and certainly more experienced, but not much wiser. Here I was, seventeen years old and acting like an adult. I had lost touch with the real me, along with my youth.

I decided to cancel all of my meetings for an entire week and on the seventh day I called Nancy to tell her I was through. I wanted to find one girl and fall in love, even at the risk it would eventually hurt me.

My situation was somewhat ironic; here I needed someone to help me find out who I was, just like the numerous ladies I always helped needed me. Who would God send to me when I needed help?

When I told Nancy I couldn't work for her anymore, she surprised me. She wasn't angry or upset. "We made a real good team, Phil. And you're leaving me with a great reputation among the ladies you were with. 'Always quit while you're still ahead, and always go out in style.' That's what I say. So will you do me one last favor—can you make me feel good by having sex with me one last time?"

I answered the way she always wanted me to, "Yes pretty lady, I will help you feel good."

When we were finished, I actually cried on her shoulder.

As *she* presented me with a red rose, Nancy said, "That is why you're so successful, you let your emotions *and* your feelings guide you. You are sensitive to others, and because of all this I am sure that you will find that one-and-only you're looking for."

Phil was good for me and for the ladies he was with. They all enjoyed his company and his special gift.

Phil had learned a lesson which many a man never does—that while most men find fulfillment in what they accomplish—women find that same feeling in satisfying relationships. I don't how he did it at such a young age, but he was "man enough" to let his feminine side come shining through, and that's what the ladies adored the most about him. Being sensitive, he knew what the ladies he met needed by actually feeling into what they secretly desired.

Whatever he decided to do next, he would succeed. I also was very positive that he would come back to me. He was too good at what he did to leave forever.

Alas, this was the first time I guessed wrong about a man. C'est la vie! Good luck Phil, wherever you go!

***

On the way home I began to question myself. How did I get into this?

I thought I was doing what I enjoyed, but I'd also begun to feel ashamed and misguided at the same time.

I felt, in a way, I was accomplishing what I set out to do when I started. I made many females like and respect me and I hoped I made every one of them feel good along the way, just like I had planned.

But even if they did feel better after spending time with me, I found myself to be thoroughly messed up and wasn't too sure what Nancy told me about finding my true love would ever come to fruition.

I needed some time alone to figure out what my next steps were going to be. The only way I could see myself figuring this out was for me to abstain from sex. I decided to concentrate on senior year and what my 'real life' would be when I got out of school. Now I just needed to convince the girls.

Chapter 35 — Terri, Revisited

Terri was the head cheerleader who taught me some of my earlier lessons. When I literally ran into her in the school hallway, she gave me a big hug and said, "There's somethin' different about you. You have this air of confidence that wasn't there the last time we met."

I agreed with her totally, but couldn't tell her why. I wish I could have, but I was having a hell of a time trying to keep the promise I made to stop having sex. In fact, I even debated calling Nancy to make some extra spending money. I couldn't tell you how, but luckily, I was able to control my urges.

We were both part of the newspaper and yearbook staffs so Terri and I started spending time together almost daily. She would always comment on my confidence level. Finally I blurted out, "Look, I'm pretty good at roller skating and the people at The Roller Wheel like me. That's where all this confidence is comin' from."

That Friday night, as I was skating, who should walk in but Terri and few of the other cheerleaders? Terri came up to me and said, "We came here to see just how good a skater you are, and why these people like you so much."

Within minutes of skating away from me she learned it all. The girls she talked to told her about my parking lot visits, my drive-in dates, and what they believed was the *real reason* why the girls liked me so much.

Terri skated back up to me and said, "Now I get it ... I see where the confidence comes from, and, I have to say, it looks real good on you."

"Thanks," I said, not really understanding what she had just told me. I became somber. "I'm tryin' to change cuz I don't like what I'm doin' anymore. I wanna get back to being just friends with these girls; it was so much easier then."

Terri gave me a long sympathetic hug and even told me she understood. Beth, one of her friends, on the other hand didn't. She wanted to experience the things she heard about. I was tired of this one-night stand ride I was on and told her so. As she left with Terri, Beth clearly was mad at me for saying no to her.

For the first time in a long time, I didn't really care what the girl thought.

Phil had changed so much since that first time I met him. He had done a complete role reversal. It actually made me think — now, I could never tell him this — it was a real turn-on. The innocent way he interacted with me, trusting me with his feelings of wanting to change, just made me even more interested. After listening to the girls at the rink, I knew I could get him to make love to me, abstinence or no abstinence.

The next Monday while we were in the newspaper classroom, Terri invited me into the darkroom so she could show me what was "developing."

We went in together and as soon as we walked into the darkness, she took my hand and put it on her breast.

I was shocked. After what I had told her in confidence last Friday night, this was the last thing I expected, and from her at that.

"Kiss me and make me feel like the others."

I wanted to honor my vow and say no, but c'mon, it's Terri, the head cheerleader.

All the feelings I had been trying so hard to suppress suddenly came to life again. I started kissing her just like I kissed everyone else. After she started to rub my upper thigh, I got a feeling I never experienced before while doing this ... it was one of regret and anger. The anger was with myself. I had made a promise to be only friends with girls and not follow through on all of my, or their, wants.

It was as if Terri had read my mind, and at that moment she pulled back.

I began to explain, "Terri, you're a great girl, I like bein' around you. This is hard for me to say, because deep down I really want to have sex with you, but can't we just be friends instead? I know I can offer you much more that way."

But I didn't need to say this. Terri had already arrived at the same decision. Still facing her, I reached behind me to open the door. As the light streaming in ricocheted off the mirror on the wall and into her eyes, I saw the one thing I always wanted to see from a girl—the sparkle of trust.

I had finally come face to face with the demons in me and won the battle. I felt as though a thousand pounds of weight had been lifted from my shoulders. The expectations I believed all girls had in me were now gone. And I felt a small spark of warmth surge through my heart.

Chapter 36 — Diane

Senior year started and I was just putting in my time. I already had all the credits I needed to graduate, so I only took one class; work for school credit. This "class" allowed me to work full time and experience the "real world."

After I got promoted to an official assistant manager, I was transferred to another Burger Shack. This actually helped me stay on the straight and narrow as I was much too busy to think about anything else.

I was now working mainly days so I met many new people, most of whom were older than I was. One of these ladies, Mildred, had a daughter, Diane, who was fifteen. Mildred was having trouble with Diane. She was hanging out with the wrong crowd. Mildred saw me as a clean cut boy who could help her daughter break out of the bad scene she was getting into. I didn't know if I believed that or not, but I reluctantly agreed to meet Mildred's daughter later that week.

The day Diane walked through the front door I thought I saw my future walk in with her. She was tall and lanky, had short blonde hair, and green eyes. Her smile was the best one I had ever seen. When I saw her dimples, I just froze with anticipation.

I also saw what her mom was concerned about when I noticed the friends she came in with. They weren't girls you'd want to associate with. Diane introduced herself, and then her friends to me and I received absolutely no response at all. But when I looked deeper into Diane's eyes, I noticed something—there wasn't the sparkle of trust *or* even the sex gleam I was used to—there was a look of wonderment and contained excitement exuding from them. It was as though she thought she might know me.

After we started to talk, her mom came up from behind me and said, "I see you've met my daughter. Isn't she pretty? She's my little princess and I try to give her everything she wants. Well, what do you think? Do you want to take her out this Friday night?"

What else could I say in front of her mom and her friends except, "Sounds good to me."

The minute I saw him I knew who he was, but I needed to contain my excitement. I told my friends to try to ignore him and act natural around my mom. I had skated many Friday nights at The Roller Wheel and watched him work his magic with the other girls. But he never knew I existed. I couldn't believe that my mom knew him and actually wanted me to date him. I already knew exactly what I wanted from him.

Misguided Sensitivity

I picked Diane up on Friday and when Mildred casually asked where we were going, Diane answered very quickly, "We're goin' roller skating, Mom, and I may be home late." She looked directly into my eyes after saying that and I saw the sex gleam boring into me like a laser.

I was flabbergasted, and when we got into the car I asked, "How do you know about The Roller Wheel?"

She flicked her hair and said excitedly, "I skate there now and then and I know all about you. I know where you go afterward, what you do there, and I want the whole package. Since you have my mom's blessing, this is gonna be so easy for me. She thinks you're a decent young man and wants me to hang with you. Little does she know what's really gonna happen?"

I shook my head at her and said, "Look, I don't do that anymore, I'm tryin' to change all that. I have made a final decision and I plan to stick to it. I know we've just met, but I really like you, and I think we may have possibilities as a couple, so I won't be taking you to the parking lot or the drive-in right now. I'd rather we take things slowly, start as friends, and see what happens."

Diane put on a pout and said, "I'll give ya two months to see where this leads us, but either way I *will* have sex with you cuz I want it and I always get what I want. I'm a little princess, ya know."

That night while we skated, Diane seemed happy to be seen with me. We went skating a few more times and each time Diane kept pushing the sex thing.

After two months, she issued an ultimatum, "Either we have sex tonight, or it's over."

When I called her bluff, she left me.

Phil was not the Phil I knew from the skating rink. He was trying to be too nice. I wanted the bad boy and he gave me the boy next door. I think because of knowing my mom he acted differently. I wanted to have sex with him so I could brag to my friends. Phil really wanted love and a long term commitment, but I just wanted sex, pure and simple. It was strange to me, wasn't it the guy who wanted a roll in the hay and then immediately forgets you? Why did he have to treat me differently than the others?

Diane was beautiful yet so naive, I knew she was rushing love, or at least the sex part of relationships and I was totally convinced she was too young to understand both of them. I didn't want to hurt her, which I knew would happen if I gave in.

For some reason, I felt God was happy with this decision and, in fact, the warm surge in my heart I normally felt after helping others became apparent to me again.

***

I wanted to be in love and lead a normal life. Diane only wanted me to treat her like the girls of my past. She wanted the parking lot, the drive-ins, and to experience the excitement of sex. When I couldn't bring myself to do that anymore a strange thought entered my head—had I finally become morally aware?

I asked myself these questions: Why couldn't Diane see everything else I had to offer? Did I bring this on myself by being with so many other girls? Was good sex really all I had to offer to women?

When I couldn't come up with any answers, I hoped and prayed something would happen to me that would explain all this.

Chapter 37 — The Greatest Lesson of All

I went home to think about my journey so far. I was almost eighteen and felt as though I had already lived a lifetime. I lay on my bed alone and recalled the ten lessons I learned early on when I made the decision to try to have every girl I met respect and like me. They were:

1) Be different, sincere, and make females feel special.
2) Girls remember and cherish the small things that they experience.
3) Girls remember the good things you do for them and want to reciprocate.
4) See the difference in everyone and celebrate it.
5) Friendship is the most important thing, it leads to other opportunities.
6) Pay attention to what a person has going on inside, not just their outside appearance or status.
7) Allow your emotions to show others you are open and caring.
8) When you truly connect with someone, age does not matter.
9) Girls want to be heard; guys need to be better listeners.
10) Girls show their trust by a sparkle in their eye.

As my life continued, I learned more lessons from the ladies I encountered. They were:

11) Always tell the truth and you won't have to remember all the lies you told.
12) Girls have the same wants and needs as guys. They think about, talk about, and want sex, and are not afraid to show their guy what gives them pleasure.
13) All good things come to an end — try to end them on a high note.
14) Be open to learning new things and trying new experiences.
15) Practice makes perfect.
16) It is better to give, but be willing to receive when it's your turn.

I poured over these lessons and reflected on the mixed results I was getting. I finally came to the conclusion they should have been an overwhelming success. So why was I *feeling* the opposite? Okay, for the most part, the women I met did like me, and most of them respected me, whether I actually felt that way now or not.

I continued to ponder this and was starting to get it. I realized the lessons weren't what were flawed; it was how I chose to use them that were questionable. This feeling sorry state I was in was brought on by no one but me and how I chose to use the special insights these ladies gave to me.

I continued to mull through all this while a new record by Rod Stewart continued to play in the background. For some reason, I always felt a real connection to his songs. He was best known for his rock songs, but if you listened to the hidden meanings in his ballads, they were often about a boy trying to find his place in this ol' world. I felt my life was a parallel to his songs.

Now, as I was closing in on eighteen, I felt as though my young life made a complete circle. I started out as introverted, very insecure, and full of self-doubt. But as I went through this process, I did become much more confident and self-assured. I paid a price by being self-centered and egotistical at times, although my intention, the whole time, was to be available to women, however they needed my help, and thus to be accepted by them.

I also came to realize every girl and every lady who I thought I was able to help along the way, had been hurt or conditioned by another man. This made me get mad at all these 'typical' guys.

I wished I could go back to a time when I was little, long before all these confusing changes occurred in my life. I wanted to go back to when life was so much simpler, and there was someone like Nana who really cared for me.

I had some real questions I needed answered. Did I use these lessons correctly? Did I truly understand what the lessons meant? Did I do the right thing by sharing what they called "my gift" with so many women? Was this actually a gift at all? Was it even a curse? What was I missing?

While I pondered these questions Rod was singing a song that really hit home—*Faith of the Heart*:

It's been a long road
getting from there to here.

Misguided Sensitivity

I'm going where my heart will lead me.
I've got faith to believe I can do anything.
Although it's been a long road,
I've got faith of the heart.

When the song ended I realized all I truly wanted from my journey were the two things we all want: to be accepted for who we are and to be happy.

But as I continued to sort through my thoughts, it came to me maybe I had used some of the ladies I met along the way only to help me feel better about myself. It then occurred to me it was possible I wasn't really thinking about them at all. And I got even more down on myself; worrying about what I had done in my past, and wanting to have it all make sense.

All this consternation was making me very confused and extremely tired. Now that I didn't know if what I had done was right, or what my next move was going to be, I wanted someone to hold me and tell me things would be fine, just like my mom did when I was little. I wanted to feel comforted again.

***

I continued to recline on my bed and thought back to the first time I saw roses at my grandmother's house and how she taught me what they symbolized. Back then, the meanings of the red and white roses were so much simpler. To me and my family, they meant love, beauty, respect, and remembrance. But as I grew up and away from my family, the symbols became more complicated, as did my life. The meaning of the white roses, in particular, changed the most.

Even with all these different meanings, I always felt like what I was doing was helping those who really needed it, and through all my experiences, I felt my intentions were always as pure as a white rose should be.

I was confused as I once again thought to myself, There has to be something I'm missing in all of this.

I can't be sure what happened next. The last thing I do remember was

I was listening to Rod sing his songs, and that's when I must have dozed off.

***

Never before, or after, have I had a dream that seemed as real as this one. I was enveloped by the strong scent of pleasing aromas which I hadn't experienced in a very long time. There was the refreshing, welcoming smell of fresh cut green grass, of hamburgers cooking over an open campfire, and the sweet smell of the early morning seaweed that always washed up on the beach. I knew in an instant I was back in Wisconsin, lying on the grassy hillside next to the cottage I loved so much when I was a young boy. I wasn't sure why I was here *or* how I got here, but I got up to see if there was anyone in the cottage. I opened the door to the front porch, and yelled out, "Is anyone home?"

But I got no response.

Then I saw the rocking chairs my Nana and I used to sit in when we talked so long ago. I slowly walked over and sat in my old chair. It felt real comfortable to me; so comfortable I began to smell another familiar scent I used to love. This scent was neither too feminine nor too masculine; it was the aroma of the sweet fertilizer my dear Nana spread throughout her rose beds. I felt safe and sound for the first time in eight years. I closed my eyes to imagine back to years gone by and when I opened them, there sitting next to me in her oversized rocking chair was my beloved Nana. Next to her was her famous lemonade, and some freshly baked desserts.

She smiled at me and said, "Well, hello, it's been a long time. Would you like some lemonade?"

I was flabbergasted and didn't understand what was happening, but as she floated a sprig of mint into two glasses of lemonade and handed one to me, I took it. Of course, I took the mint out of mine and put it into my pocket.

Nana asked, "So, what brings you around today?"

I felt a gentleness and comfort in her voice, so I said, "I'm so lost and lonely right now, I don't know what to do. I have no idea if how I'm living my life is right or wrong. I just wanted to help others, be respected, and be happy, but I don't know if I'm goin' about it correctly."

Nana let loose with a gentle smile of understanding. "We know."

"We?" I said. "Who are we? It's only you and me here."

She shook her head no. "We are me and God. You should never feel alone, we are always there right next to you. We've been part of all the twists and turns, ups and downs, and confusion in your life. It's all been an opportunity for growth. This life phase you are in is all about learning, sharing, and helping. And I have to say, my dearest Phil, you worry too much."

"How can you say that?" I shook my head in disbelief. "I've had sex, drank, stretched the truth, and even was angry at God sometimes. How can you say I shouldn't worry?"

Nana took my hand. "Do you remember when we talked about religion when you were young, and I told you it didn't matter how or where you worshiped God, as long as you kept your faith?"

I nodded yes.

"Well, you have and you do," she said. "You are helping spread the messages of joy, happiness, and forgiveness every day. The lessons you have chosen to live by have helped you navigate your way in a sometimes complicated world."

I was stunned. "How'd you know about my lessons?"

"Who do you think was giving them to you?"

I was confused. "But why am I doing things many people would call immoral?"

The answer I got came as a surprise.

"I can't tell you why you do the things you do. Only you can. I can tell you though, in your own special way, you are there for those who need you the most, and that's what living this life is all about: helping others, respecting them, and in turn, building a relationship with God," Nana explained. "In return for this, you get love and respect back. God has always been there to help you understand all this. As one of many signs, every time you feel a warm feeling surge through your heart, it reaffirms the Spirit is around."

"God believes in you, and is a fair and good God who works in miraculous ways. And although you may not always understand what the Lord does, you need to trust that everything happens for a reason.

Your *unique way* of helping, may not be the preferred way, but God still understands."

Nana stopped to take a drink of lemonade, and to let everything she said soak into my tiny little brain.

"So far in your young life you have made a great difference to those you've met. Although, you've been so busy helping *them* you have forgotten about yourself. Sometimes, you must stop and help yourself along the way."

She smiled and it made me relax as she continued her sermon. "And although you may think sex is the gift you have been given, you couldn't be more wrong. Sex, used in the correct way can be a pleasure, but it doesn't always equate to happiness. The *real gift* you were given so long ago is the ability to be sensitive to those you meet. Because you use it often, we know you not only understand the difference between what is right and wrong, but that the people you share it with understand your intentions are good. God understands you have sometimes gone against your better judgment, so if you need the Lord to forgive you—"

Nana suddenly turned and looked upward. "Hey, do you smell that?"

I did, and I knew what it meant. It was the smell of a storm coming in. As the rain started to gently pour down, Nana and I went out to the hillside and once again began dancing together, just like we used to when I was a kid. While we moved to our own beats, she said, "If this isn't God sending you a sign that says 'I love you, I forgive you, and I really care about you,' then I don't know what is."

I closed my eyes and spun around in the blissful rain, feeling like a young boy again.

***

When I opened my eyes, I was back in my bed listening to Rod sing his songs I loved so much. I wondered if in my dream I actually traveled to another dimension and spent some time with Nana. But it really didn't matter, because that's when the answer I was searching for came to me.

This journey—this life with all the people and symbols I had experienced—made me realize what the sign in my grandmother's dining room, "God Works in Miraculous Ways," actually meant.

The Lord had shown me, in a special way, life continues on through the good and the bad, and each and every person you meet along the way leaves pieces behind, just like a jigsaw puzzle, in order for you to piece together as you grow and learn. And as you put the various pieces together, you hopefully become a better person for it.

We are indeed all connected, and everything you do really does matter, and it will always affect someone else in one way or another.

Self-discovery, in this life phase, is an on-going journey, and the number one priority is to learn from it. God was showing me, even though I didn't realize it at the time that our whole entire human life is a symbol, and there is no such thing as an ending, only new beginnings. The circle of life never ends, even in what we call death.

And as I felt my whole body begin to warm because of God's presence, this became my greatest lesson of them all: *God is always there, loving and guiding you through.*

***

When I went to take my clothes off to fall back asleep, a few things fell out of my pants pocket. A smile came to my face as I looked down at a sprig of mint, along with a few rose pedals—both white and red ones. I assumed the white ones were there to remind me to keep an open mind, and do my best to always have a pure heart; while the red ones let me know that, even through the misguided choices I made, God still loved me. These mementos reaffirmed a saying my grandmother once told me: *All roses have thorns.* But now I knew you could work through them if you're careful and see beyond what people perceive as the obvious.

And thanks to the beautiful ladies I met, to my Nana, and especially because of God, I truly believed I could go on practicing the lessons I learned to become a healthy, productive, well-liked male. Only this time, I would use better judgment.

***

Just before I drifted off to sleep, a soft voice, which was neither male nor female, but very calm and soothing, said to me:

Pleasure is relative. Happiness is absolute. It is the understanding and acceptance of life as it is. You now know that you are accepted for who you are, so go and be happy.

I truly hoped that I could. But I was still very young and knew I wasn't done learning yet. I fell asleep wondering what was next for me on this journey of self-discovery called life.

About the Author

Philip Nork was born in Chicago, Illinois and is the oldest of three children. His early years were devastating as he endured the divorce of his parents, the death of his beloved great-grandmother, and the resulting feelings of isolation and loneliness. While these events took their toll, they also shaped the man he grew up to be.

Phil had a different perspective than his friends and his experiences were totally unique. As his young male friends were busy playing baseball, defending their turf, and hitting on girls, his time was spent reading, listening to music, writing his feelings down in his journal and trying to understand the differences in people and to figure out how "we can all get along."

After graduating early from high school, he entered the work force as a way to help support his mother and his siblings. To get away from the reality of his life, Phil spent much of his off time with his friend Joyce, a lesbian. She was able to help him experience women at his own pace and taught him many of the lessons he was to put in place. As more and more straight ladies entered his life, these experiences allowed him to learn more about human nature and he was able to turn these special times into the stories in his book.

Phil lives in Nevada with his wife and their son. He mixes work with his love of writing. He spent the first 25 years of his working life in the restaurant industry. He took all the knowledge from his early days at McDonalds and parlayed that into a successful stint with Panera Bread. He rose from the day to day operations of a general manager to become an Area Manager and then a Training Manager for that organization. Teaching and speaking in front of hundreds of trainees day in and day out helped him perfect his easy going style. He is now an Area Manager for CDS, a marketing and sales firm which specializes in working with the vendors of Costco Wholesale Warehouses.

In addition to writing, Phil is a baseball card collector, an avid reader, and enjoys listening to the music of his youth, especially Rod Stewart and Air Supply.

ALL THINGS THAT MATTER PRESS ™

FOR MORE INFORMATION ON TITLES AVAILABLE FROM
ALL THINGS THAT MATTER PRESS, GO TO
http://allthingsthatmatterpress.com
or contact us at
allthingsthatmatterpress@gmail.com

www.ingramcontent.com/pod-product-compliance
Lightning Source LLC
Chambersburg PA
CBHW071713090426
42738CB00009B/1756